2nd Workshop on Creative-text Translation and Technology (CTT 2025)

Geneva, Switzerland
24 June 2025

ISBN: 979-8-3313-2671-5

Printed from e-media with permission by:

Curran Associates, Inc.
57 Morehouse Lane
Red Hook, NY 12571

Some format issues inherent in the e-media version may also appear in this print version.

Association for Computational Linguistics
209 N. Eighth Street
Stroudsburg, Pennsylvania 18360

Phone: 1-570-476-8006
Fax: 1-570-476-0860

acl@aclweb.org

Additional copies of this publication are available from:

Curran Associates, Inc.
57 Morehouse Lane
Red Hook, NY 12571 USA
Phone: 845-758-0400
Fax: 845-758-2633
Email: curran@proceedings.com
Web: www.proceedings.com

ctt 2025

Second Workshop on Creative-text Translation and Technology (CTT)

Proceedings of the Workshop

June 24, 2025

Geneva, Switzerland

Message from the Organising Committee

In this volume, we present the contributions to the second edition of the Workshop on Creative-text Translation and Technology (CTT).[1] The CTT workshop was co-located with the 20th Machine Translation Summit (MT Summit 2025)[2] and was held on 24 June 2025 in Geneva, Switzerland.

Scope Continuing the first edition of CTT, we explored the interaction between translation technology and creativity. As neural machine translation (NMT) and large language models (LLMs) become increasingly prominent in translation workflows, new questions emerge about their role in creative translation tasks, where nuance, cultural sensitivity, and stylistic variation are key. Our call for papers welcomed contributions from researchers, translators, educators, and developers alike, with a focus on how such technologies can support or challenge creative processes in contexts such as literature, poetry, video games, marketing, and audiovisual translation. We encouraged submissions that address both technological innovation and its integration into practice, with the aim of engaging in a multidisciplinary discussion around creativity and language technology.

Submissions We received eight submissions in total. Each submission was reviewed by three reviewers in a double-blind peer-review process. One paper was submitted to another workshop co-located with MT Summit and after deliberation with the organizers, it was decided that the paper was better suited there. After careful evaluation, five out of the seven remaining papers were accepted for oral presentation, resulting in an acceptance rate of 71.4%. The accepted papers cover a broad range of topics and approaches, reflecting the diversity of the field and the growing interest in creative translation and technology.

A number of papers focus on the evaluation and perception of machine-generated translations. Li and Daems examine how the perceived source of translation affects revision quality, especially across different genres. Mikelenić, Oliver, and Àlvarez Vidal present RomCro v2.0, an expanded multilingual corpus for fine-tuning NMT systems on literary texts, and demonstrate improvements in fluency and style when using this corpus. Kong and Macken conduct a stylometric analysis of Peter Pan translations, comparing outputs from LLMs, NMT systems, and human translators, and show that LLMs align more closely with human translation style than NMT systems.

In terms of workflows and tools, Macken, Daems, and Ruffo compare translation strategies across different modes: human translation, CAT tools, and post-editing, with an emphasis on how each handles translation difficulties in literary texts. Finally, Brenner and Othlinghaus-Wulhorst investigate how domain-adapted machine translation affects the user experience of video game translators, highlighting a clear preference for flexible post-editing workflows over static use of generic MT output.

Together, the contributions in this volume reflect central questions of the workshop: how translation technologies interact with creative practice, where their strengths and limitations lie, and how translators experience and adapt to these tools in their workflows. We hope these proceedings offer valuable insights into the evolving relationship between creativity and language technology.

Keynotes We had the pleasure to host two keynote speakers at this edition of CTT.[3] **Marion Botella**, Associate Professor in Differential Psychology at Université Paris Cité, provided a keynote presentation titled "The creative process according to psychology and methods to explore it" on how creativity is studied and defined in Psychology, with a focus on the stages and mechanisms of the creative process and

[1]https://ctt2025.ccl.kuleuven.be/
[2]https://mtsummit2025.unige.ch/
[3]https://ctt2025.ccl.kuleuven.be/keynotes

the methods used to observe and evaluate it. **Tim Van de Cruys**, Associate Professor in the Department of Linguistics, Faculty of Arts, KU Leuven, presented "Modeling linguistic creativity for computational literary translation", introducing his ERC project TENACITY and the challenges involved with modeling creativity from a computational perspective.

Sponsors CTT was kindly sponsored by INTERACT: Interdisciplinary research network on language contact research[4], which is funded by the Research Foundation Flanders (FWO) with grant number W002220N. The Faculty of Arts and Philosophy of Ghent University (UGent) sponsored CTT as well.

Bram Vanroy
Marie-Aude Lefer
Lieve Macken
Paola Ruffo
Ana Guerberof Arenas
Damien Hansen

[4] https://interact.ugent.be/

Organising Committee

Bram Vanroy	KU Leuven, Belgium & Dutch Language Institute (INT), The Netherlands
Marie-Aude Lefer	UCLouvain, Belgium
Lieve Macken	Ghent University, Belgium
Paola Ruffo	Ghent University, Belgium
Ana Guerberof Arenas	Groningen University, The Netherlands
Damien Hansen	Université libre de Bruxelles, Belgium

Programme Committee

Alina Karakanta	University of Leiden, The Netherlands
Antoni Oliver Gonzàlez	Universitat Oberta de Catalunya. Spain
Antonio Toral	University of Groningen, The Netherlands
Arda Tezcan	Ghent University, Belgium
Chantal Wright	Zürcher Hochschule für Angewandte Wissenschaften, Switzerland
Dorothy Kenny	Dublin City University, Ireland
James Hadley	University of Dublin, Trinity College, Ireland
Kristiina Taivalkoski-Shilov	University of Turku, Finland
Leena Salmi	University of Turku, Finland
Lucas Nunes Vierira	University of Bristol, United Kingdom
Lynne Bowker	University of Ottawa, Canada
Marion Winters	Heriot-Watt University, United Kingdom
Minna Ruokonen	University of Eastern Finland, Finland
Pilar Sanchez Gijon	Autonomous University of Barcelona, Spain
Sheila Castilho	Dublin City University, Ireland
Susana Valdez	University of Leiden, The Netherlands
Vilelmini Sosoni	Ionian University, Greece
Waltraud Kolb	Universität Vienna, Austria

Keynote Talk

The Creative Process According to Psychology and Methods to Explore it

Marion Botella
Université Paris Cité

Abstract: According to psychology, creativity is the ability to produce ideas that are both original and appropriate (Lubart et al., 2015). Fitting in with this definition, the creative process is then the sequence of thoughts and actions that result in an original and adapted production. This process can thus be described according to a macro approach, detailing the stages that make it up, or by a micro approach, detailing the mechanisms within each stage. In this presentation, we will define creativity and, more specifically, the creative process according to psychology, and then look at the methods used to evaluate or observe it.

Bio: Marion Botella is associate professor in Differential Psychology at Université Paris Cité. After defending her thesis describing how emotions are involved in the artistic creative process, she was post-doctoral researcher at the UCLouvain (Belgium) where she examined the impact of creativity on mood. Since 2013, she is conducting her research within the Applied Psychology and Ergonomic Lab (LaPEA). Her research focus on (1) the creative process in various domains (as art, design, science, ...), (2) the teaching of creativity, (3) the development and construction of scales. Her research often involves mixed methods, both quantitative and qualitative.

Keynote Talk

Modeling Linguistic Creativity for Computational Literary Translation

Tim Van de Cruys
Faculty of Arts, KU Leuven

Abstract: Literary translation poses unique challenges for computational systems - not only in terms of preserving meaning, but in conveying tone, imagery, and style. Creativity plays a central role, especially when translating texts that resist straightforward alignment. In this talk, I present the ERC project TENACITY, which explores unsupervised models of linguistic creativity using tensor-based semantic representations and neural network architectures. These models do not merely replicate language patterns, but aim to understand and generate language with creative intent. I explore how such models can contribute to the task of literary translation, particularly when dealing with metaphor, ambiguity, or stylistic shifts - offering computational techniques that complement the work of human translators in capturing linguistic nuance.

Bio: Tim Van de Cruys's main research interest is natural language processing, with a particular focus on the unsupervised modeling of meaning, the analysis of multivariate language data within the mathematical framework of tensor algebra, and creative language generation. He is currently an associate professor with the Linguistics Department at the Faculty of Arts, KU Leuven. Previously, he was a CNRS researcher affiliated to the IRIT computer science laboratory in Toulouse. He obtained his PhD from the University of Groningen, and held post-doctoral positions at INRIA in Paris, and the University of Cambridge.

Table of Contents

The Role of Translation Workflows in Overcoming Translation Difficulties: A Comparative Analysis of Human and Machine Translation (Post-Editing) Approaches

Lieve Macken, Paola Ruffo and Joke Daems
Department of Translation, Interpreting and Communication
Ghent University
Belgium
{firstname.lastname}@ugent.be

Abstract

This study investigates the impact of different translation workflows and underlying machine translation technologies on the translation techniques used in literary translations. We compare human translation, translation within a computer-assisted translation (CAT) tool, and machine translation post-editing (MTPE), alongside (unedited) neural machine translation (NMT) and large language models (LLMs). Using three short stories translated from English into Dutch, we annotated potential translation difficulties and the translation techniques that were employed to overcome them. Our analysis reveals differences in translation solutions across modalities, highlighting the influence of technology on the final translation. The findings suggest that while MTPE tends to produce more literal translations, human translators and CAT tools exhibit greater creativity and employ more non-literal translation techniques. Additionally, LLMs reduced the number of literal translation solutions compared to traditional NMT systems. While our study provides valuable insights, it is limited by the use of only three texts and a single language pair. Further research is needed to explore these dynamics across a broader range of texts and languages, to better understand the full impact of translation workflows and technologies on literary translation.

1 Introduction

A growing body of work is trying to understand how the experience of a reader is influenced by the characteristics of the (translated) text they are reading, and how those characteristics are in turn influenced by the translation process. For example, a low quality translation, where a translator exerted limited effort, was found to be harder to read than a high quality translation of the same source text (Whyatt et al., 2023). A translation's quality might, in part, be influenced by the extent to which a translator successfully handles elements in the source text that require creative solutions, i.e., elements that cannot be easily reproduced in the target language. Introducing more so-called creative shifts in a translation does not automatically lead to higher quality, but knowing when to introduce a creative shift versus when to 'settle for' a more literal reproduction of the source does (Bayer-Hohenwarter, 2011). More experienced translators also exhibit a wider range of translation strategies compared to novices (Dyachuk, 2014). Especially in the context of literary text, where creative use of language is the norm rather than the exception, the way translation problems are handled by a translator is likely to influence the reader's experience.

In modern translation workflows, the translator is not the only factor to take into account, however. Even for literary translation, translators sometimes make use of CAT tools (Youdale and Rothwell, 2022) and the potential of machine translation (MT) is actively being explored (Hansen and Esperança-Rodier, 2022). The use of MT has been shown to negatively impact creativity for literary texts compared to human translation, even after post-editing (Guerberof-Arenas and Toral, 2022). Large language models (LLMs) are increasingly being used for translation as well, although they also seem to lead to products of reduced creativity compared to human translation (Zhang et al., 2024).

With the present work, we aim to improve our understanding of how different translation workflows can lead to differences in translation products for literary texts translated from English into Dutch. We start by identifying the textual units in the source texts that represent potential translation problems requiring creative solutions. Understanding translation problems is crucial from a translation process perspective, as they can lead to increased cognitive effort (Bayer-Hohenwarter, 2011). Additionally,

Proceedings of the Second Workshop on Creative-text Translation and Technology (CTT), pages 1–13, June 24, 2025

the way translation problems are handled is likely influenced by access to technology, with MT potentially solving some problems but introducing new ones (Nitzke, 2019). From a translation product perspective, it is crucial to understand how differences in process lead to differences in product, as those differences are likely to lead to different reader experiences. More specifically, this study aims to answer the following research questions:

- RQ1: What are the typical English-Dutch translation problems for which non-literal translation techniques are used?
- RQ2: How do the translation techniques used differ between different translation modalities? (e.g. human translation, translation in a CAT tool and post-edited machine translation)?
- RQ3: How do the translation techniques used differ between neural machine translation systems and those based on large language models?

It should be noted that, over the years, different authors have used different terms to refer to the concept of translation techniques. We use the terminological distinctions articulated by Molina (2002) and use the term 'translation strategy' to refer to the mechanisms used by translators throughout the translation process to find a solution to the problems they face (for example a target-language oriented strategy), and the term 'translation technique' to refer to the result achieved in the translation product, which can be identified in the micro-units of the text. In the following sections, we first briefly introduce some of the work on translation difficulties and translation techniques, as well as their relationship to creativity, and the potential impact of translation technology. We then outline our methodology, results, and end with a discussion and conclusion summarising our main findings.

2 Related work

2.1 Translation difficulty and translation techniques

In translation studies, the term 'difficulty' can refer both to the cognitive effort involved in completing a task and the inherent difficulty of the task itself (Sun, 2015). Difficulties in translation can be of various kinds, including culture-specific problems, text-specific problems and challenges arising from changes in the communicative situation (such as differences in place, time and the prior knowledge of the target language reader). Translation-specific difficulties often occur when there is a lack of equivalence between source and target language: something that can be expressed a certain way in one language but not in the other (Sun, 2015; Reiss, 1983). It is important to note, however, that the perception of difficulty is influenced by the expertise and language skills of the translators themselves and is to some extent subjective.

In the field of product-oriented translation studies, extensive research has been conducted on equivalence and translation techniques. In their seminal work, Vinay and Darbelnet (1958) introduced a taxonomy of translation procedures[1], distinguishing between direct procedures (resembling word-for-word translations) and oblique procedures, employed when literal translation is inadequate. Zhai et al. (2018) annotated translation relations[2] in a trilingual parallel corpus (English, French, and Chinese) using a categorisation scheme inspired by Vinay and Darbelnet's taxonomy and used this dataset to train a classifier that can distinguish between literal translations and other translation relations (Zhai et al., 2019).

2.2 Translation solutions and creativity

The idea of non-literal translations has been linked to the notion of creativity. Bayer-Hohenwarter (2011) labeled source text elements as having a low or high creative potential based on whether or not they could be reproduced easily in the target language and then studied how translation students and professionals handled those elements. Instances of abstraction, concretisation, and modification were considered to be 'creative shifts'. There is considerable overlap between these categories and those defined by Zhai et al. (2018). The author found individual differences across participants and revealed that translators often apply creative strategies even for elements that can be reproduced almost literally (Bayer-Hohenwarter, 2011). She further stresses that increased creativity does not necessarily lead to increased quality, as translators can introduce creative shifts that contain errors, but that creativity is an indicator of translational flexibility.

[1] Vinay and Darbelnet used the term 'translation procedures' to refer to what we understand as 'translation techniques'.

[2] Zhai and colleagues used the term 'translation relations'.

2.3 Impact of technology on translation solutions and creativity

The use of translation technology can have an impact on the translation process and product (Doherty, 2016). Working with a CAT tool can ensure that translators do not skip sentences and produce consistent translations, but can feel limiting in the sense that translators are forced to work sentence-by-sentence, especially where literary translation is concerned (Daems, 2022). Post-editing MT output has been shown to be cognitively less effortful than translating from scratch, suggesting that it offers some solutions to translation problems (Nitzke, 2019), yet MT output might also lead to decreased creativity. The specific style of a literary translator has been shown to be impacted by the use of MT output (Winters and Kenny, 2023). Furthermore, the quality of MT output depends on the source text, with certain literary texts proving more challenging than others, and MT output follows source text structures much more closely than human translations do (Webster et al., 2020; Vanmassenhove et al., 2021). The usefulness of MT also depends on the level of equivalence between source and target language. When translating multi-word units (MWU) between English and Dutch, for example, MT produces more errors for contrastive MWUs, and these are also harder to post-edit (Daems et al., 2018).

Inspired by Bayer-Hohenwarter, Guerberof-Arenas and Toral (2022) explored 'units of creative potential' in a literary source text (which they define as units that require the translators to use their high problem-solving capacity as opposed to those that are regarded as routine units that are standard in the translation practice) and found that human translations led to higher creativity scores compared to MT output and post-edited texts. In later work, they explored the impact of these differences in creativity on reader experience and found differences between Catalan and Dutch readers, with Catalan readers preferring HT over MT(PE) and Dutch readers preferring the original or sometimes the PE version over the HT version (Guerberof-Arenas and Toral, 2024). This indicates that while there is a relationship between translation workflow and creativity as well as between creativity and reading experience, this relationship is mediated by additional factors (such as reading language, language status, individual translators, and translation quality) that require more research to be properly understood.

Previous work comparing the impact of translation workflow (human translation, CAT tool, post-editing) on textual characteristics in literary texts for English-Dutch showed that features such as sentence length, sentence alignment and lexical diversity were not as dissimilar between conditions as anticipated, but did indicate that certain MTPE texts were stylometrically similar to the original MT output, additionally suggesting that a more in-depth analysis of translation solutions is necessary to better understand these differences and similarities (Daems et al., 2024).

An additional factor to take into account is the potential influence of LLMs in future automated workflows. Recent work on Chinese-English literary translation suggests that ChatGPT produces more accurate and nuanced translations than DeepL (Sun, 2024). By performing a stylistic analysis using classification and clustering techniques on English-Chinese children's literature, Kong and Macken (2025) show that certain LLMs are closer to human translation than to NMT, but also report performance variability between LLMs. A study comparing four different languages also found that LLMs outperformed NMT systems for literary translation (Zhang et al., 2024). On the other hand, the authors stress that human translations are still more diverse and less literal than LLM translations (Zhang et al., 2024). When used as an automated post-editing tool for literary texts, ChatGPT was found to fix fewer MT errors than human translators and also introduced additional problems in the final text (Macken, 2024). These findings suggest that as LLMs are likely to be used more in future literary translation workflows (given their potential improvements over NMT), it also becomes increasingly important to gain a better understanding of their limitations when it comes to handling translation problems.

3 Methodology

3.1 Data

In this study, we use a subset of the data collected in the DUAL-T project (Ruffo et al., 2024), consisting of Dutch translations of three short stories (*Rome*, *The Beautiful Girl in the Bookstore*, and *They Kept Driving Faster and Outran the Rain*) from the 2014 collection *One More Thing* by the American author B. J. Novak. The stories present elements of satire, humour, and absurdity, offering a critique of modern life. These stories (approx. 950 source words in total) were translated by twenty-four experienced professional literary translators under three different conditions: (1) conventional translation using a word processing tool (Microsoft Word), (2) translation within a computer-assisted translation (CAT) environment using Trados Studio 2022, and (3) post-editing of a machine translation output.

Short stories were selected as the source texts because they are self-contained, manageable within a single session, and still pose a meaningful challenge for professional literary translators. Additionally, the stories needed to be part of an English-language collection with an existing Dutch translation, allowing for the creation of a translation memory (TM) containing the other short stories from *One More Thing* for use in the Trados Studio 2022 condition.

The experimental sessions were conducted either at Ghent University or at Leiden University. Each session took place in a lab and typically lasted 4 to 5 hours. Participants were supervised by one of the study's authors, received a flat fee of €250 for their participation, and were reimbursed for travel expenses. After reading an information letter and signing a consent form, participant received a translation brief instructing them to translate the texts to the best of their ability, aiming for a quality as close to publishable as possible within the given experimental constraints.

For our analysis, we selected the translations produced by the nine most experienced translators, ensuring that each text had nine versions, with three translations per condition (three human translations, three post-edited versions and three CAT versions). The machine-translated versions used as the starting point for the post-editing task were generated in July 2023 using the commercial neural machine translation system DeepL.

We enriched the DUAL-T dataset by adding the published Dutch translation available for this collection (*Onverzameld Werk*, published by Agathon in 2014 and translated from English by Jevgenia Lodewijks, Lydia Meeder and Maarten van der Werf). In addition to the DeepL translation, we included two translations generated by two large language models (LLMs) in order to compare the performance of LLMs with neural machine translation (NMT). The LLM translations were produced using GPT-4o and Unbabel 7B in December 2024, following the simple prompt to "translate the text into Dutch". The final data set thus consists of 13 versions of each of the three source texts.

	T1	T2	T3	Total
Multiword	34	23	13	70
Compounds	7	5	1	13
Fixed expr.	12	6	4	22
Idiomatic expr.	1	2	0	3
Light-verb constr.	1	0	2	3
Verb-particle constr.	13	10	6	29
Complex structure	20	12	12	44
Noun phrase	4	3	4	11
Syntactic structure	16	9	8	33
Cultural & linguistic variant	0	3	0	3
Cultural references	0	1	0	1
Linguistic variant	0	2	0	2
Colloquial language	4	2	7	13
Metaphor & original image	0	2	5	7
Total	**58**	**42**	**37**	**137**

Table 1: Overview of the different translation problems identified in the three texts

3.2 Potential translation problems

To annotate potential translation problems, we adopted a comprehensive and non-restrictive approach. We included all categories related to the 'units of creative potential' proposed by Guerberof-Arenas and Toral (2020). In addition, based on the work of Sun (2015), various types of multiword items, complex noun phrases and complex syntactic structures were included. Using this combined classification list, a total of 137 units were selected. The different types of problems identified in the three source texts are summarised in Table 1.

3.3 Translation techniques

To annotate the translation techniques, we slightly adapted the classification scheme of Zhai et al. (2018) and added an 'untranslated' category (see Appendix A[3] for all labels and their explanation). To improve the feasibility of the annotation task, and contrary to the approach of Zhai et al., we only annotated translation techniques for the potential translation problems identified in the first step.

To facilitate the annotation process, annotations were made using LabelStudio. Annotation guidelines[4] were developed based on the framework established by Zhai et al. The annotation work was carried out by a student with a degree in languages and literature, who is currently enrolled in a Masters in Translation. This student annotated all the texts, working in a sentence-by-sentence

[3]As the typology builds on the work of Zhai et al. (2018), we originally adopted their term 'translation relations' in our typology and in LabelStudio.

[4]The annotation guidelines are available upon request.

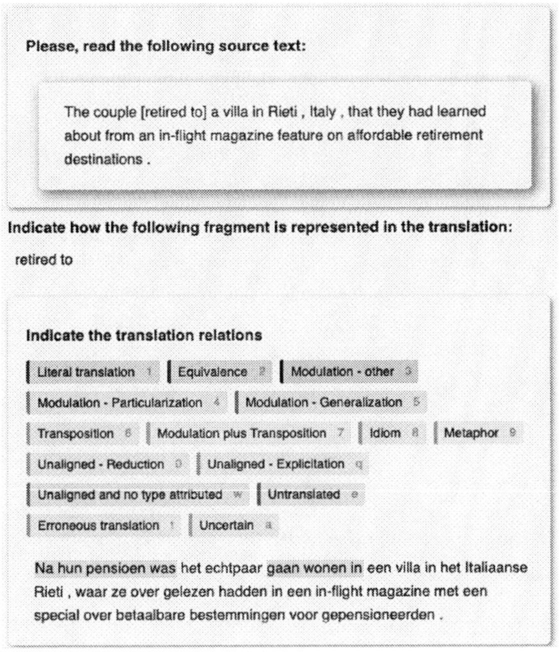

Figure 1: Annotation of translation techniques in Label Studio

view (source sentence followed by its respective translations for all translation modalities). For each potential translation problem, the student selected the corresponding translations and identified one or more translation techniques. Figure 1 presents an example of one annotation step. In this example, the verb-particle construction *'retired to'* is translated as *'na hun pensioen was ... gaan wonen in'* (En: *'After their retirement ... had gone to live in'*). This translation was labeled as 'Modulation plus Transposition' because part of the meaning of the verb *'retired'* is expressed in the prepositional phrase (transposition), and the point of view has been changed as well (modulation).

The student maintained a record of difficult annotations. These difficult cases were subsequently reviewed and discussed with one of the authors, leading to refinements in the annotation guidelines based on their discussions. A total of 2,225 translation techniques were identified in the 39 translations (see Table 2), which corresponds to 33 hours of annotation work.

During the annotation process, a total of 14 errors were identified across all translations. Nine of these errors were found in translations done by professionals, which could be attributed to the limitations of the experimental conditions in which the translations were produced. It should also be noted that the manual annotation process only focused on potential translation problems, rather than evaluating the translations in their entirety.

	T1	T2	T3	Total
Literal	334	321	221	876
Equivalence	223	142	197	562
Non-literal	283	139	163	585
Particularization	60	53	32	145
Generalization	46	21	22	89
Mod. other	90	43	30	163
Transposition	68	13	56	137
Mod. + Trans.	19	9	21	49
Metaphor	0	0	2	2
Unaligned	61	32	31	124
Reduction	31	19	13	63
Explicitation	23	11	7	41
No type attributed	7	2	11	20
Erroneous	4	7	3	14
Untranslated	5	19	8	32
Uncertain	9	15	8	32
Total	**919**	**675**	**631**	**2225**

Table 2: Overview of all labelled translation techniques in the three texts

4 Results

4.1 English-Dutch translation difficulties requiring non-literal translation techniques

To answer RQ1, we adopt the hierarchy of translation techniques of Zhai et al. (2018), categorizing the translation techniques into four groups (literal, non-literal, equivalence and unaligned) by aggregating the different categories of modulation, transposition, idiom and metaphor into one group 'non-literal'. Figure 2 shows the percentage of different groups per potential translation problem. From this figure we can see that more than 60% of the cases in the problem categories 'linguistic variant', 'institutionalised phrases' and 'compound nouns' were translated literally. Thus, these categories do not pose significant translation problems when translating from English into Dutch. Conversely, the categories 'colloquial language', 'complex syntactic structure', 'metaphor and original image', and 'verb-particle constructions' presented the lowest percentages of literal translation solutions and can thus be considered the most challenging cases. It should be noted that some categories did not occur frequently in the source texts (e.g. there were only three 'idiomatic expressions' and three 'light verb constructions', see Table 1), so some results should be interpreted with caution.

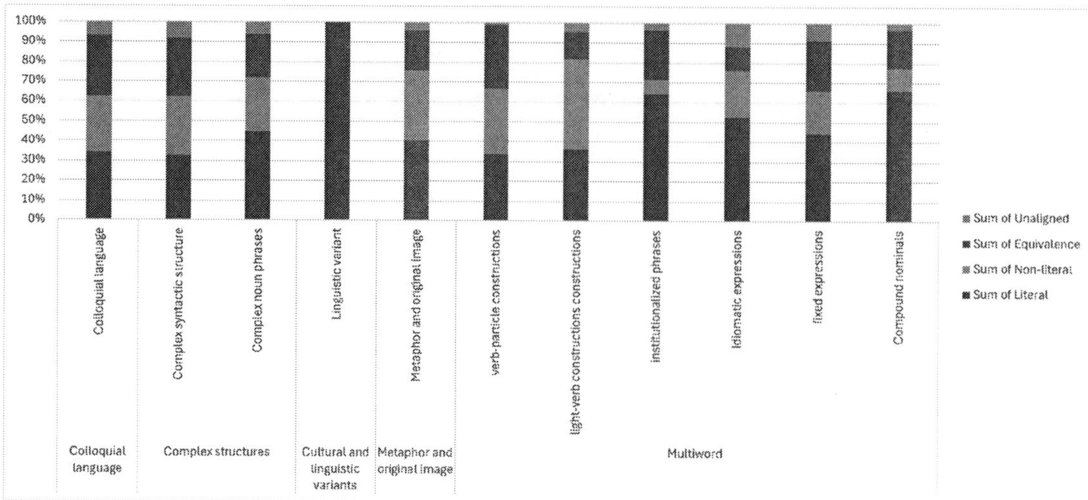

Figure 2: Percentage of different translation techniques per translation difficulty category

EN	She loved the kind of books you could buy in stores **that also sold things**.
MT	Ze hield van het soort boeken dat je kon kopen in winkels **die ook dingen verkochten**.
MTPE	Ze was dol op de boeken die je kon krijgen in van die winkels **die ook spullen verkochten**.
HT	Ze hield van het soort boeken dat je kon kopen in winkels **waar ook andere spullen werden verkocht**.
EN	It was about fifty minutes outside of Rome by car . . .
MT	Het was ongeveer vijftig minuten buiten Rome met de auto . . .
MTPE	Het lag op zo'n vijftig minuten rijden van Rome . . .
HT	**Vanuit Rieti** was het ongeveer vijftig minuten rijden naar Rome . . .

Table 3: Examples of 'modulation - other' and 'explicitation' in the human translation

4.2 Translation techniques across translation modalities

To address RQ2, we aggregated the translation techniques per translation condition across participants and texts. As can be seen in Figure 3, the post-edited texts contain the highest proportion of literal translation techniques compared to translations produced using a CAT tool or human translations produced using MS Word. In contrast, HT and CAT outputs displayed a greater use of non-literal techniques, with 'modulation - other' and 'particularisation' being the most frequently applied techniques in these conditions (see Figure 5 in Appendix B).

Looking more closely at the unaligned translations, we found that professional literary translators used more explicitations as a translation technique in the human translation condition (see Figure 6 in Appendix B), while reduction was the preferred technique in both the CAT and MTPE conditions. This could suggest that translators may be more inclined to elaborate on ambiguous or culturally specific elements when not constrained by a CAT tool text segmentation or by a pre-existing MT output.

In Table 3, we give two examples, in which the professional literary translator resp. used the non-standard translation technique of 'modulation' and 'explicitation'. In the first example, the source sentence contains a construction with a non-human agent as subject in English ('stores'), which is a construction that occurs frequently in English, but less so in Dutch. DeepL produced a very literal translation, which was edited in the post-editing condition, but the English construction was retained. The professional translator changed the perspective (HT: *winkels waar ook andere spullen werden verkocht*; En: *shops in which other stuff was also sold*). In the second example, the machine translation again produced a very literal translation, which was improved during post-editing. However, in the MS Word translation, the professional translator explicitly added the place of departure (*vanuit Rieti*; En: *from Rieti*), which was mentioned earlier in the text.

Nevertheless, when examining translation techniques across the three texts, the picture becomes less clear-cut. For example, Figure 7 in Appendix B illustrates considerable variation in translation techniques within the HT condition. However, it is possible to discern similar patterns in relation to each text. For example, T3 presents more inci-

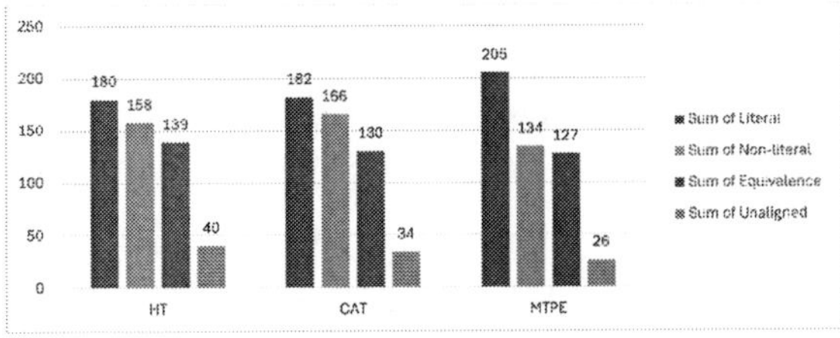

Figure 3: Number of different types of translation techniques across translation modalities

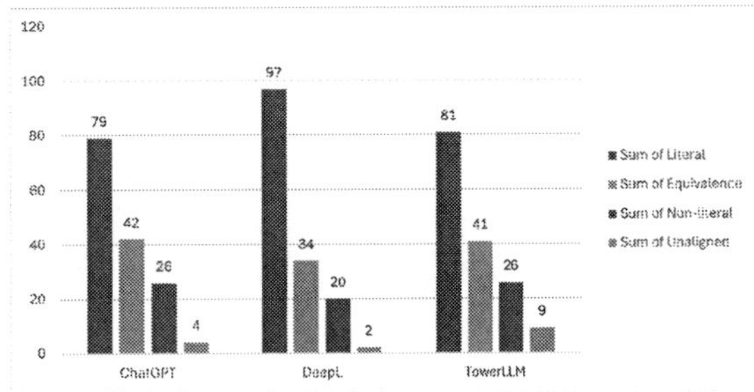

Figure 4: Translation techniques per MT system across text

dences of equivalence and non-literal translations when compared to T2, where literal translations are the most common translation technique among all three translators in the HT condition, while more variability can be observed for T1.

Figure 8 shows considerable variation in translation techniques among individual translators. The published translation used as reference presented the lowest number of literal translation techniques. However, it is worth noting this may be attributed to the additional revision step in the publishing process.

Figures 9, 10 and 11 in Appendix B further show how text-specific characteristics might have had an impact on translation techniques. In particular, T1 (Figure 9) presents more pronounced differences between both the three translation conditions and individual translators. Conversely, the differences between T2 (Figure 10) and T3 (Figure 11) are less substantial. More specifically, for T2 literal translations were the preferred translation technique for all participants across all translation conditions. T3 presents more instances of equivalent and non-literal techniques in the HT and CAT conditions, while literal solutions are consistently higher in the MTPE workflow. Overall, these patterns seem to also be reflected in the reference translation. This suggests that the relationship between translation condition and translation techniques is mediated by both individual translator preferences and specific textual characteristics.

4.3 Translation techniques in NMT and LLMs

To answer RQ3, we look at the different translation techniques for each of the three MT systems. Figure 4 shows that the NMT system produced more literal translation techniques than the two LLM systems. The distribution of translation techniques between the two LLM systems is virtually identical, with both systems producing slightly more equivalent and non-literal solutions when compared to the NMT system.

5 Discussion & Conclusion

To gain a better understanding of how different translation workflows influence translation products, we looked at potential translation problems and their solutions across different translation modalities (HT, CAT, MTPE, NMT, LLMs). To identify potential translation problems we relied on prior work on translation difficulties/challenges (Sun, 2015; Guerberof-Arenas and Toral, 2024). To categorize the translation techniques employed across various translation modalities, we used the classification framework developed by Zhai et al. (2018). We manually labelled all translation problems and translation techniques. This was a very time-consuming process. Future work could explore the potential of LLMs to identify translation problems and translation techniques.

Overall, the machine translation generated more literal translation solutions when compared to the HT or CAT translation condition. This aligns with previous research showing that NMT systems produce more literal translations and follow the structure of the source language more closely (Webster et al., 2020; Vanmassenhove et al., 2021). While post-editing slightly reduces the number of literal translation solutions when compared to raw MT and LLM output, the overall degree of literal translation techniques remained higher in the MTPE condition. This suggests that the initial machine translation output influences the final translation, with translators potentially hesitant to make substantial creative changes to the machine-provided solutions, which is in line with the findings of Castilho and Resende (2022) and Kolb (2024).

Our findings also revealed individual variations among professional translators working in the post-editing condition. This confirms earlier results from a cluster analysis using bootstrap consensus trees in Stylo, which showed that most MTPE translations clustered together and showed some stylometric similarity with the MT output. However, some MTPE translations did not belong to the MTPE cluster, indicating that certain translators made more significant changes (Daems et al., 2024).

In addition, individual text characteristics were shown to have a considerable impact on translation techniques across all conditions. In fact, our analysis revealed varying patterns of translation techniques for each text, suggesting that certain textual features may present different types of translation challenges that influence translator decisions regardless of the workflow. This highlights the importance of considering text type and specific source text features when evaluating the potential benefits of different translation technologies.

It is also worth noting that our study focused on post-edited NMT output, whereas our comparative analysis suggests that LLMs produce less literal translations than traditional NMT systems. This raises the possibility that post-editing LLM-generated translations might lead to a reduction of literal translation techniques compared to MTPE.

To conclude, while our study provides valuable insights into how different translation workflows affect translation relations for literary texts, it also highlights the fact that the interplay between individual translator preferences, source text characteristics, and translation technology deserves further investigation, particularly as LLM-based translation continues to develop. More research is needed on individual variation among professional translators.

Acknowledgments

This research was conducted within the framework of the DUAL-T project, which has been granted financial support from the European Union's Horizon Europe (HORIZON) research and innovation programme under the Marie Skłodowska-Curie grant agreement No 101062428.

References

Gerrit Bayer-Hohenwarter. 2011. "creative shifts" as a means of measuring and promoting translational creativity. *Meta*, 56(3):663–692.

Sheila Castilho and Natália Resende. 2022. Post-editese in literary translations. *Information*, 13(2):66.

Joke Daems. 2022. Dutch literary translators' use and perceived usefulness of technology: The role of awareness and attitude. In *Using technologies for creative-text translation*. Taylor & Francis.

Joke Daems, Michael Carl, Sonia Vandepitte, Robert J Hartsuiker, and Lieve Macken. 2018. How do students cope with machine translation output of multiword units? an exploratory study. In *Multiword Units in Machine Translation and Translation Technology*, pages 61–80. John Benjamins Publishing Company.

Joke Daems, Paola Ruffo, and Lieve Macken. 2024. Impact of translation workflows with and without MT on textual characteristics in literary translation. In *Proceedings of the 1st Workshop on Creative-text Translation and Technology*, pages 57–64, Sheffield, United Kingdom. European Association for Machine Translation.

Stephen Doherty. 2016. The impact of translation technologies on the process and product of translation. *International journal of communication*, 10:23.

Nataliya Dyachuk. 2014. Psycholinguistic features of creative literary translation. *East European Journal of Psycholinguistics*, 1(2):7–14.

Ana Guerberof-Arenas and Antonio Toral. 2020. The impact of post-editing and machine translation on creativity and reading experience. *Translation Spaces*, 9(2):255–282.

Ana Guerberof-Arenas and Antonio Toral. 2022. Creativity in translation: Machine translation as a constraint for literary texts. *Translation Spaces*, 11(2):184–212.

Ana Guerberof-Arenas and Antonio Toral. 2024. To be or not to be: A translation reception study of a literary text translated into dutch and catalan using machine translation. *Target*, 36(2):215–244.

Damien Hansen and Emmanuelle Esperança-Rodier. 2022. Human-adapted mt for literary texts: Reality or fantasy? In *NeTTT 2022*, pages 178–190.

Waltraud Kolb. 2024. "Quite puzzling when I first read it": Is reading for literary translation different from reading for post-editing? *Palimpsestes. Revue de traduction*, (38).

Delu Kong and Lieve Macken. 2025. Can Peter Pan Survive MT? A Stylometric Study of LLMs, NMTs, and HTs in Children's Literature Translation. In *Proceedings of the 2nd Workshop on Creative-text Translation and Technology*, Geneva, Switzerland.

Lieve Macken. 2024. Machine translation meets large language models: Evaluating ChatGPT's ability to automatically post-edit literary texts. In *Proceedings of the 1st Workshop on Creative-text Translation and Technology*, pages 65–81, Sheffield, United Kingdom. European Association for Machine Translation.

Amparo Molina, Lucía ; Hurtado Albir. 2002. Translation techniques revisited: A dynamic and functionalist approach. *Meta*, 47(4):498–512.

Jean Nitzke. 2019. *Problem solving activities in post-editing and translation from scratch: A multi-method study*. Language Science Press.

Katharina Reiss. 1983. Adequacy and equivalence in translation. *The Bible Translator*, 34(3):301–308.

Paola Ruffo, Joke Daems, and Lieve Macken. 2024. Measured and perceived effort : assessing three literary translation workflows. *Revista Tradumàtica. Tecnologies de la Traducció*, (22):238–257.

Rui Sun. 2024. Evaluating the Translation Accuracy of ChatGPT and DeepL Through the Lens of Implied Subjects. *Arab World English Journal For Translation and Literary Studies*, 8(4):41–53.

Sanjun Sun. 2015. Measuring translation difficulty: Theoretical and methodological considerations. *Across Languages and Cultures*, 16(1):29 – 54.

Eva Vanmassenhove, Dimitar Shterionov, and Matthew Gwilliam. 2021. Machine translationese: Effects of algorithmic bias on linguistic complexity in machine translation. In *Proceedings of the 16th Conference of the European Chapter of the Association for Computational Linguistics: Main Volume*, pages 2203–2213, Online. Association for Computational Linguistics.

Jean-Paul Vinay and Jean Darbelnet. 1958. *Stylistique comparée du français et de l'anglais: méthode de traduction*. Didier, Paris.

Rebecca Webster, Margot Fonteyne, Arda Tezcan, Lieve Macken, and Joke Daems. 2020. Gutenberg goes neural: Comparing features of Dutch human translations with raw neural machine translation outputs in a corpus of English literary classics. In *Informatics*, volume 7, page 32. MDPI.

Bogusława Whyatt, Olga Witczak, Ewa Tomczak-Łukaszewska, and Olha Lehka-Paul. 2023. The proof of the translation process is in the reading of the target text: An eyetracking reception study. *Ampersand*, 11:100149.

Marion Winters and Dorothy Kenny. 2023. Mark my keywords: a translator-specific exploration of style in literary machine translation. In *Computer-Assisted Literary Translation*, pages 69–88. Routledge.

Roy Youdale and Andrew Rothwell. 2022. Computer-assisted translation (cat) tools, translation memory, and literary translation. In *The Routledge handbook of translation and memory*, pages 381–402. Routledge.

Yuming Zhai, Gabriel Illouz, and Anne Vilnat. 2019. Classification automatique des procédés de traduction. In *26th Conférence sur le Traitement Automatique des Langues Naturelles*.

Yuming Zhai, Aurélien Max, and Anne Vilnat. 2018. Construction of a multilingual corpus annotated with translation relations. In *Proceedings of the First Workshop on Linguistic Resources for Natural Language Processing*, pages 102–111, Santa Fe, New Mexico, USA. Association for Computational Linguistics.

Ran Zhang, Wei Zhao, and Steffen Eger. 2024. How good are LLMs for literary translation, really? literary translation evaluation with humans and LLMs. *arXiv preprint arXiv:2410.18697*.

A Appendix: typology of translation techniques

Translation technique / Translation relation	Explanation
Literal translation	Word-for-word translation (including insertion or deletion of determiners, changes between singular and plural forms), or possible literal translation of some idioms; the underlying syntactic construction is similar in both languages
Equivalence	Non-literal translation of proverbs, idioms, fixed expressions or syntactical constructions (which cannot be transferred as such into the target language) OR semantic equivalence at the supra-lexical level, translation of terms
Modulation - Particularization	The translation is more precise or presents a more concrete sense
Modulation - Generalization	The translation is more general or neutral OR translation of an idiom by a non-fixed expression OR removal of a metaphorical image
Modulation - Other	Changing the point of view, either to circumvent a translation difficulty or to reveal a way of seeing things
Transposition	Translating words or expressions by using other grammatical categories (e.g. noun → verb) than the ones used in the source language, without altering the meaning of the utterance
Modulation plus Transposition	Any sub-type of Modulation combined with Transposition
Idiom	Translate a non-fixed expression by an idiom
Metaphor	Keep the same metaphorical image by using a non-literal translation OR introduce metaphorical expression to translate non-metaphor
Unaligned - Reduction	Remove deliberately certain content words in translation
Unaligned - Explicitation	Introduce clarifications that remain implicit in the source language
Unaligned – no type attributed	Translated words which don't correspond to any source words
Erroneous translation	Obvious translation error
Untranslated	Keep the source in the target to avoid the translation problem
Uncertain	Difficult example (not clear from annotation guidelines how to annotate this example)

B Appendix: Additional figures

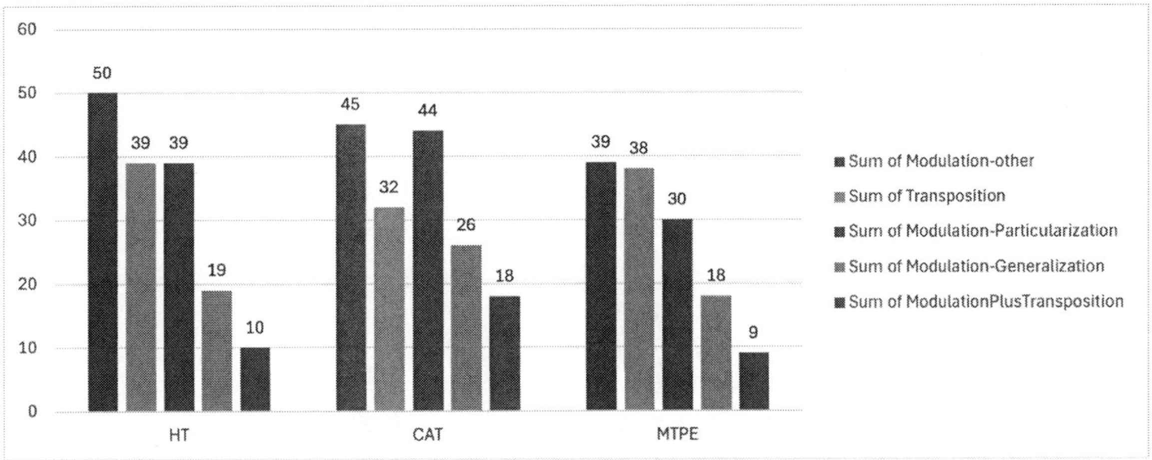

Figure 5: Number of different non-literal translation techniques across translation modalities

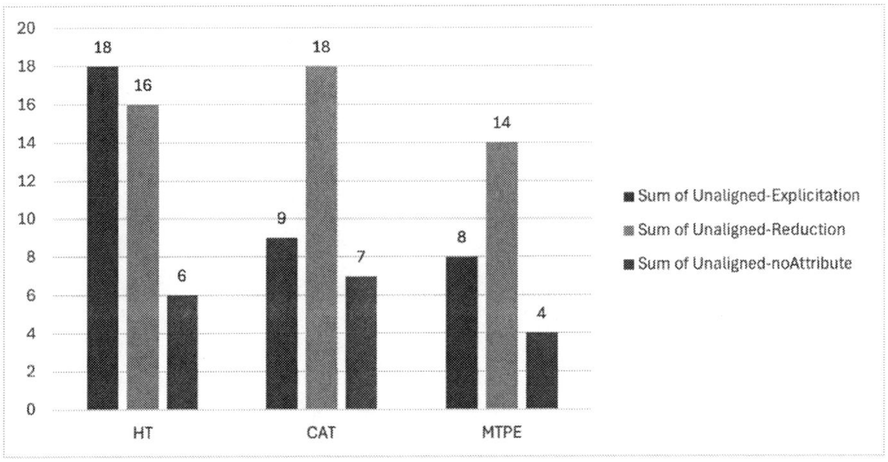

Figure 6: Number of different unaligned translation techniques across translation modalities

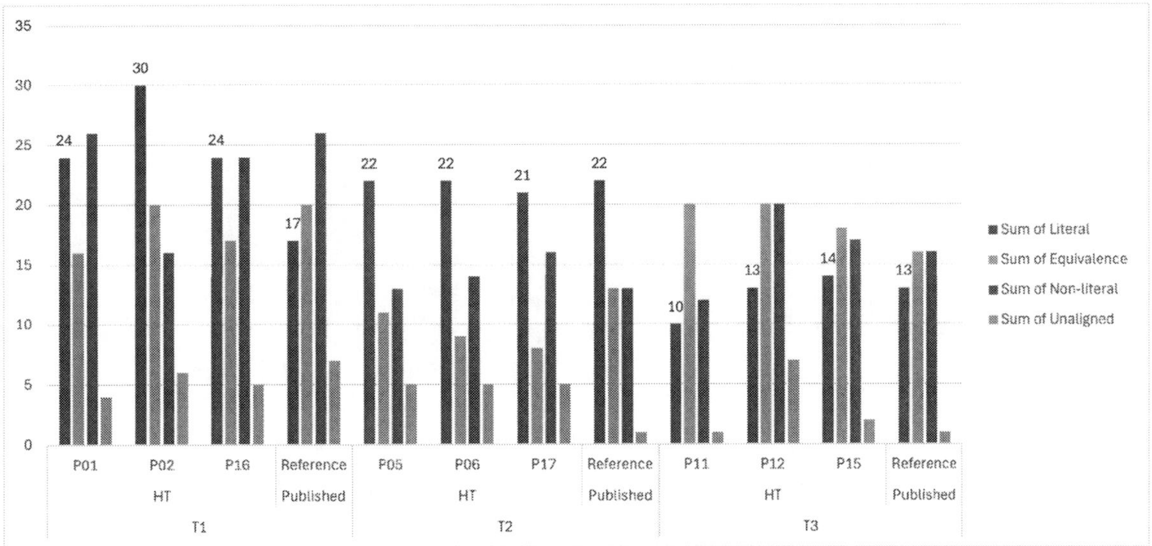

Figure 7: Translation techniques per text and participant, HT condition only

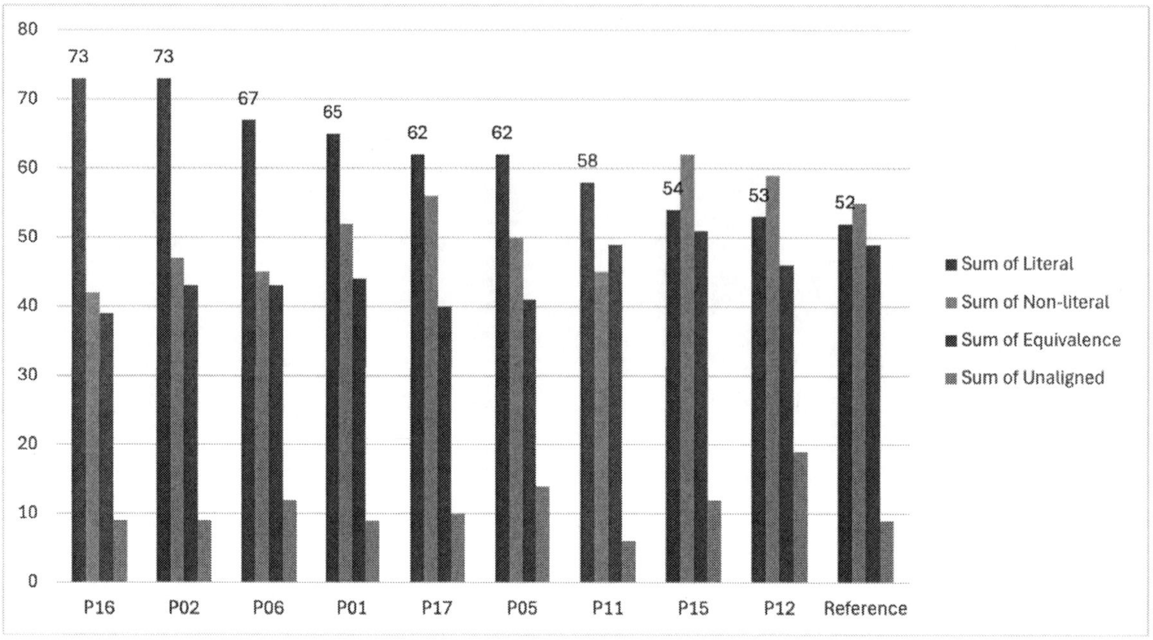

Figure 8: Translation techniques per participant across texts and conditions

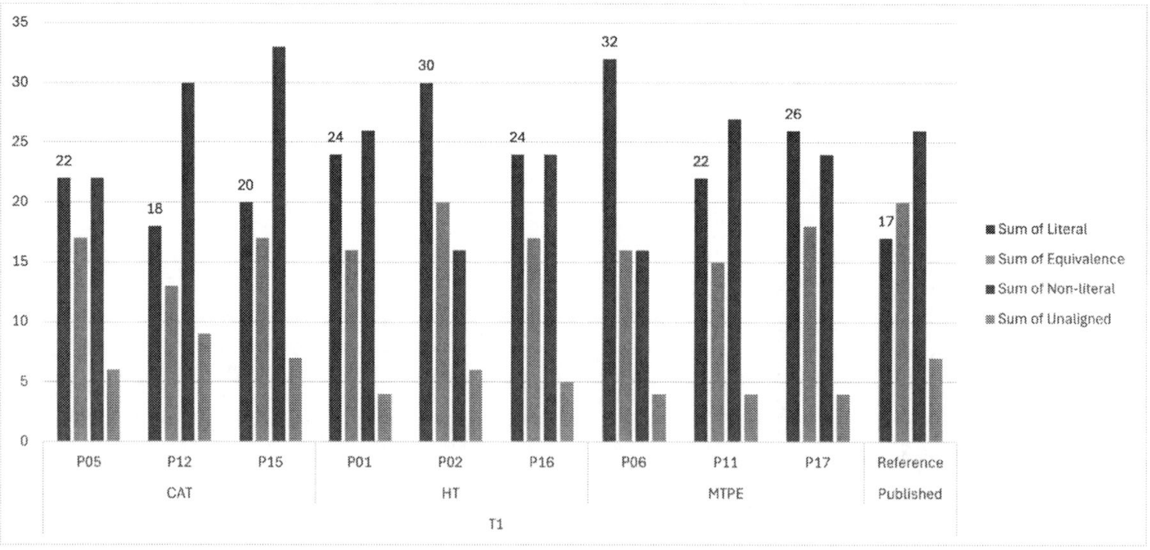

Figure 9: Translation techniques for Text 1

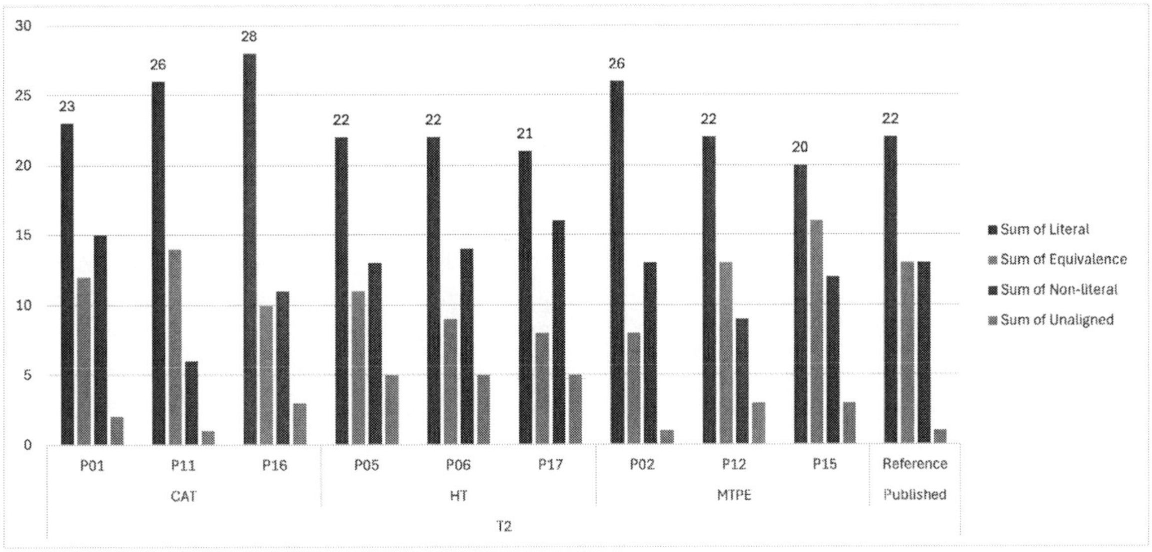

Figure 10: Translation techniques for Text 2

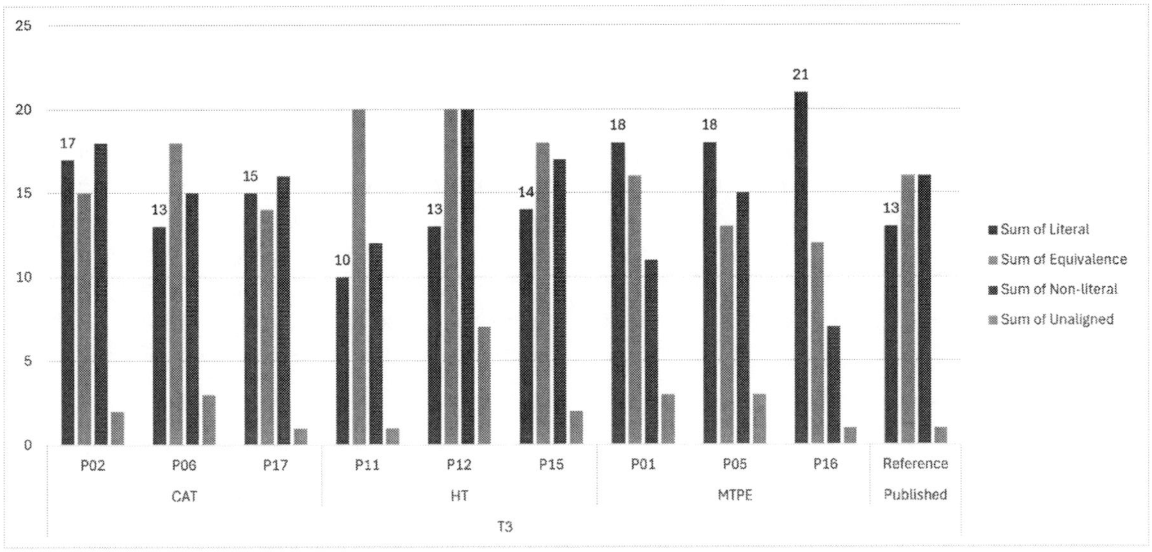

Figure 11: Translation techniques for Text 3

Does the perceived source of a translation (NMT vs. HT) impact student revision quality for news and literary texts?

Xiaoye Li
Hunan University / Changsha, China
Ghent University / Ghent, Belgium
lixiaoye2022@hnu.edu.cn

Joke Daems
Ghent University / Ghent, Belgium
joke.daems@ugent.be

Abstract

With quality improvements in neural machine translation (NMT), scholars have argued that human translation revision and MT post-editing are becoming more alike, which would have implications for translator training. This exploratory study contributes to this growing body of work by exploring the ability of 16 student translators (ZH-EN) to distinguish between NMT and human translation (HT) for news text and literary text and analyses how text type and student perceptions influence their subsequent revision process. We found that participants were reasonably adept at distinguishing between NMT and HT, particularly for literary text. Participants' revision quality was dependent on the text type and the perceived source of translation. The findings also highlight student translators' limited competence in revision and post-editing, emphasizing the need to integrate NMT, revision, and post-editing into translation training programmes.

1 Introduction

The rise of neural machine translation (NMT) has led to paradigm shifts in translation research and education. Claims of NMT quality reaching 'human parity' (Hassan et al., 2018), suggest blurring boundaries between MT and human translation (HT). While this claim has been contested (Läubli et al., 2020; Poibeau, 2022), it has had consequences for text types considered to be suitable for MT and for the conceptualisation of revision and post-editing (PE). With quality improvements over earlier MT paradigms, a growing body of work has explored the potential of NMT for literary translation (Matusov, 2019; Toral and Way, 2018), and some book publishers are actively integrating post-editing into their workflows (Creamer, 2024).

From a theoretical perspective, the evolution in MT quality sparked a debate on the fundamental differences between post-editing (the improvement of machine-translated text) and revision (the improvement of human-translated text), and whether they have essentially become the same task (Do Carmo and Moorkens, 2020). Such distinctions (or lack thereof) are important from a translation training perspective, as students need to develop the necessary skills to thrive in the translation industry. If post-editing and revision are fundamentally different tasks, students need to receive training explicitly tailored to both (Robert et al., 2024). It has been suggested that being able to identify differences between HT and NMT output is a key component of MT literacy (De Clercq et al., 2021). An additional factor is the potential lack of transparency in the translation workflow itself. When receiving a revision assignment, translators might not always be made aware of the actual provenance (machine or human) of a translation, and they will still be required to produce a final text fit for publication.

In order to improve our understanding of (perceived) differences and similarities between NMT and HT, this study evaluates the ability of student translators to distinguish between both for two distinct text types: news text and literary text. Students were asked to clarify their choices and to edit the text to produce a final product of publishable quality. In this paper, we answer the following research questions:

RQ1. Can students distinguish between NMT-translated or human-translated texts for different text types?

RQ2. Which factors do students take into account when determining the source of translations and do they consider different factors for different text types?

RQ3. Does the source of a translation and whether or not it is correctly identified influence the

Proceedings of the Second Workshop on Creative-text Translation and Technology (CTT), pages 14–26, June 24, 2025

changes students make? That is, will the number of revision changes and the revision quality be higher when participants correctly identify the source of the translation?

2 Related research

2.1 NMT for different text types

NMT represents a new paradigm in the field of machine translation (MT), demonstrating substantial improvements in translation quality (Koponen et al., 2021). Existing studies have shown the promising performance of NMT for technical text (Wang and Wang, 2021), yet its effectiveness for creative texts remains unclear. Creative texts, shaped by human creativity and reliant on aesthetics, traditionally include genres like novels, poetry, plays, and comics (Hadley et al., 2022). Although news texts are informational in nature, they still offer a certain degree of creative space, especially when conveying cultural nuances and subtleties. Due to the need for rapid information delivery (Yang et al., 2023), NMT has been adopted in news translation (Krüger, 2022; Dai and Liu, 2024). In comparison to news texts, literary texts require a higher level of creativity, and there is an ongoing debate about NMT's applicability to literary works (Daems, 2022; Guerberof-Arenas et al., 2024; Rothwell et al., 2023). Studies showed that around 30-44% of sentences in NMT outputs for literary texts do not contain any errors (Matusov, 2019; Tezcan et al., 2019; Toral and Way, 2018) and that there is a great variability in error types depending on the language pair, with morphosyntactic errors being particularly common for French-to-Croatian, and literal translations and lexical errors being common for English-to-French translations (Petrak et al., 2022).

2.2 Differences between NMT and HT

While quality is a crucial component to judge the potential of NMT for different text types, the impact of technology on language as a whole is a topic of discussion as well. Research into so-called Machine Translationese has shown that the use of MT leads to a loss of linguistic, morphological and syntactic diversity compared to original texts or human translations (Vanmassenhove et al., 2019, 2021; De Clercq et al., 2021; Tezcan et al., 2019; Bizzoni et al., 2020; Sizov et al., 2024). Understanding the impact of MT on language becomes particularly important in the context of literary translation, where creativity is a key component. For classic novels translated from English into Dutch, for example, NMT was shown to have a lower level of lexical diversity than HT, and HT showed more syntactic variability, whereas NMT output generally followed the source text structure (Webster et al., 2020). Research on literary translation for English-Turkish (Şahin and Gürses, 2019) and English-Catalan and English-Dutch (Guerberof-Arenas and Toral, 2022) revealed that NMT negatively impacts creativity, which could also influence the readers' experience. Idioms and manipulated multiword expressions can pose a particular challenge to NMT compared to human translators (Corpas Pastor and Noriega-Santiáñez, 2024).

2.3 Translation revision and post-editing

The ISO 17100 (2015) explicitly states that translation services should ensure that translations are revised. It underscores the critical role of revision in enhancing the quality of human-translated texts. Similarly, post-editing is an essential step in ensuring the final quality of NMT-translated texts. Numerous researchers have engaged in theoretical discussions on translation revision and post-editing (Do Carmo and Moorkens, 2020; Nitzke et al., 2019; Robert et al., 2017; Scocchera, 2020).

Theoretically, some scholars argue that post-editing can be regarded as a form of revision, as it may be carried out monolingually without access to the source text (Krings, 2001; Schwartz, 2014). This view is further supported by evidence that translators spend more time pausing than typing during post-editing tasks (Koehn, 2009; Ortiz-Martínez et al., 2016).

However, this viewpoint has been contested. Jakobsen (2018) notes that while technology blurs the boundaries between translation, revision, and post-editing, fundamental differences between human and machine translation distinguish the latter two. Similarly, do Carmo and Moorkens (2020) caution that perceiving post-editing as a form of revision might lead to its undervaluation and influence pedagogical practices. Girletti (2022) found that corporate translators in Switzerland regard revision and post-editing as separate tasks, despite similarities in reading strategies. Evidence from a literary translation workflow in which an MT text was first post-edited and then revised indeed shows that the kinds of changes introduced in both processes are very different (Macken et al., 2022), with post-editing actions mostly focusing on the correction of MT errors, and revision actions focusing on preferential changes (explicitation, stylistics changes, coherence markers).

The debate about the differences and similarities between translation revision and post-editing has an impact on translator training, and the (presumed) necessary competences for both. Some scholars have proposed different competence frameworks for revision and post-editing, respectively (Pym, 2013; Rico Pérez and Torrejón, 2012; Robert et al., 2017; Scocchera, 2020; Konttinen et al., 2020). It suggests that earlier theoretical discussions are still not settled, and previous conclusions are still being examined through practical research.

To date, few studies have empirically verified the differences between translation revision and post-editing, and the data analysed in existing studies have been limited to translations between European languages, such as English-Dutch (Daems and Macken, 2020) and Dutch-French (Robert et al., 2023). Daems and Macken (2020) conducted a study in which professional translators were asked to revise or post-edit a given source text, with some 'revisors' being given an MT source text, and some 'post-editors' being given a HT, without the translators being aware of this deception. The study showed that most changes were made to the MT text when participants thought they were revising a HT, and that this also led to the greatest quality improvements. Robert, Schrijver and Ureel (2023) focused on competences in translation trainees to establish if there are differences between translation, translation revision, and post-editing. They concluded that revision is different from post-editing as students performed worse for the post-editing task, although the 'problem detection' competence was found to be shared across both tasks.

Therefore, this study aims to examine the perceived similarities and differences between NMT and HT, and to determine whether the perceived source of translations affect the revision quality across news and literary texts. Moreover, it will be the first to explore the relationship between translation revision and post-editing across languages that are more distant and linguistically remote from each other, i.e. Chinese and English.

3 Methods

3.1 Participants

Participants were 16 students enrolled in a Translation and Interpreting Master program from Hunan university in China. They were native Chinese speakers (L1) with English as their second language (L2). All participants had passed the Test for English Majors at Band 8, a standardized English proficiency exam in Chinese universities, ensuring a high level of English proficiency. Translation into English is a core competence in Chinese translator education due to market demands. Participation in the experiment was optional as part of the students' translation course, with participation leading to extra course credit. The experiment was approved by the Ethics Committee of the School of Foreign Languages at Hunan University. All participants signed an Informed Consent form before the experiment.

To minimize the impact of English proficiency on the experimental results, we used R Studio to run a greedy algorithm that divided participants into two groups: Group A and Group B. The greedy algorithm is used to optimize resource allocation with minimal variance between groups (Korte and Vygen, 2018), and we used it to ensure that the overall English proficiency of the two groups was as balanced as possible (see Table 1).

Indicators	Group A	Group B
Participants	8	8
EN proficiency	86.00	86.13
Age	21.70	21.50
Task 1	HT of prose	NMT of prose
Task 2	NMT of news	HT of news

Table 1: Information of Group A and Group B

3.2 Materials

3.2.1 Source texts

When selecting the source text (ST), we comply with the following requirements. First, the total length of the ST should be kept within a specified range to prevent participant fatigue from excessively long texts. Second, the average sentence length of the ST should be regulated, as NMT performs better with shorter sentences (Moorkens et al., 2018). This ensured that NMT outputs were not overly refined, which could reduce the need for post-editing (Daems et al., 2017). Third, text complexity should be evaluated via objective and subjective methods. The objective evaluation method could take into account linguistic features such as sentence structure (Hvelplund, 2011). The subjective evaluation method involves translator experts to assess the readability, comprehensibility, and translatability of texts (Zheng et al., 2020).

Based on these requirements, We firstly selected four source texts (two from a news text and two from a literary text), ensuring consistency in the number of Chinese characters and sentences. Then, four translators with over five years of experience evaluated the text complexity across readability, comprehensibility, and translatability using a Likert scale (1 = easy, 5 = difficult).

After evaluation, we selected two Chinese source texts (ST 1 and ST 2) for the formal experiments. ST 1 was drawn from a news text titled 'The Belt and Road Initiative: A Key Pillar of the Global Community of Shared Future' published by The State Council Information Office of the People's Republic of China. ST 2 was excerpted from a Chinese literary text titled 'Time Is Life' by Shiqiu Liang, a well-known Chinese writer. It conveyed the author's thoughts on time and life, characterized by rich rhetorical devices. After evaluation, ST 1 and ST 2 predominantly consist of complex sentences such as progressive compound sentences or sequential compound sentences. Both texts share a similar number of Chinese characters, average sentence length, and closely aligned results in subjective evaluations (see Table 2). These results suggest that the two texts are comparable in terms of text complexity.

Indicators	ST 1	ST 2
Text genre	news text	literary text
Number of characters	131	123
Number of sentences	4	4
Avg. sentence length	32.75	30.75
Readability	3.50	3.55
Comprehensibility	3.00	3.10
Translatability	3.85	3.80

Table 2: Information of ST 1 and ST 2

3.2.2 Sources of translations

The source texts were translated from scratch by a senior undergraduate student majoring in English. The student was instructed to translate without using NMT or consult any online resources.

To simulate real-world scenarios where translators assess translation outputs from various NMT systems, we translated the STs using several widely accessible and reliable NMT systems, including Google Translate, DeepL, Baidu Translate, and Youdao Translate.

The quality of these HT and NMT outputs was then evaluated by two professional translators, with more than 10 years of translation experience, using Multidimensional Quality Metrics (MQM) (Lommel et al., 2014) alongside reference translations. The reference translation of the literary text was by Peiji Zhang, a renowned Chinese translator, while the news translation was adopted from the China State Council Information Office. Following Carl and Baez (2019), translation errors could be classified into two categories: 'critical' errors (score of 2) and 'minor' errors (score of 1).

Based on the evaluation results, we selected the translations by DeepL for PE tasks, as they were the most similar to HT in terms of the number of errors. This was done to prevent the imbalance in the number of errors between NMT and HT from affecting the results. Since the number of errors in the NMT-translated literary text was one more than in the HT-translated literary text, We then corrected one minor fluency error in the DeepL translation to ensure consistency in both the number of errors and the error severity weight between the human-translated and NMT-translated texts. After the adjustment, the final translations contained 8 errors with a total error severity weight of 14. A full overview of error types for each text and translation source can be seen in Appendix A.

3.3 Experiment procedure

To initiate the experiment, we provided participants with a task brief, post-editing guidelines (Nitzke and Hansen-Schirra, 2021), and general revision guidelines (Moorkens et al., 2018), followed by the distribution of the experimental tasks. These supplementary materials can be found online at `https://osf.io/ubc8x/?view_only=f11dc93134004f01a029b207415b02d2`. All participants installed EVCapture, a screen recording software, on their laptops and completed a warm-up exercise to practice revision and post-editing.

During the formal experiments, participants were instructed to complete two tasks (Task 1 and Task 2). We used a between-subjects design, with each participant receiving one ST in its HT version and the other in its NMT version (participants were not informed of the origin of the translations). The details of group division are shown in Table 1. The current design was implemented to minimize potential biases that could arise from asking participants to identify both HT and NMT of the same ST. Such a task might have influenced their judgment and revision quality in two ways: First, participants could have compared the two translations while making their assessment. Second, having access to both translations might offer helpful hints during the revision or post-editing process.

For each task, participants were instructed to identify the source of translations, provide the rationale behind their perceptions, revise the translations, and explain the reasons for their changes. There was no time limitation and participants were permitted to use online resources. Given that English translations of the STs were available at the time, we instructed participants not to consult any English versions during the experiment. Furthermore, all participants' translation processes was recorded by EVCapture. Upon completing the tasks, participants needed to save their revised documents and screen recording files.

3.4 Data collection and evaluation

This study utilized Microsoft Word documents to gather participants' perceived sources of translations, their criteria for judgment, revised translations, and the reasons for their revision changes. The accuracy rate of participants' perceived translation sources was calculated based on the perception results documented in the Word files.

The coding process for the judgment criteria was conducted across four scenarios: NMT of news text, HT of news text, NMT of literary text, and HT of literary text. Each scenario was classified as either 'consistent' or 'inconsistent', depending on whether the perceived source aligned with the actual source. 'Consistent' refers to instances where participants' perceptions matched the true source, whereas 'inconsistent' denotes cases where there was a discrepancy. In light of participants' comments, thematic keywords for each judgment criterion were identified, with care taken to minimize overlap between themes. Two main thematic keywords were identified: all comments could be classified as either relating to translation strategies or to errors. For instance, P01 noted that 'the translation is too literal' in the NMT of news text, which was categorized under the thematic keyword 'translation strategies'. Similarly, P01's comments in the HT of literary text, 'this translation even includes a spelling error,' was categorized under 'translation errors'. The frequency of each thematic keyword was then collected to identify the primary criteria participants used to assess the source of the translations across different scenarios.

For revision changes, six types of changes proposed by Robert et al. (2018) was categorised into two groups. The first group consists of changes made to translation segments with errors, which were further divided into 'necessary changes', 'missed necessary changes', and 'underrevisions'. The second group encompasses changes made to error-free translation segments, classified as 'overrevisions' (or error introduction), 'hyperrevisions' (or unnecessary changes), and 'improvements'. Two professional translators with more than 10 years of translation experience were invited to classify the revision changes based on these categories and were compensated for their time. Any disagreements in classification were resolved through discussion with the authors of this study.

Revision quality was calculated using the formula proposed by Daems and Macken (2020), focusing on three key metrics: 'necessary changes', 'overrevisions', and 'total number of errors'. Changes for critical errors, which greatly impact quality, were assigned a severity weight of '2', while those for minor errors, with less impact, were assigned '1'. The revision quality is calculated using the following formula:

$$\text{Revision Quality} = \frac{(NC \times SW) - (OR \times SW)}{TNE \times SW}$$

where:

- NC = Necessary Changes
- OR = Overrevisions
- SW = Severity Weight
- TNE = Total Number of Errors

3.5 Data analysis

Descriptive statistics were calculated for the accuracy rate of perceived sources of translations and revision changes, with the mean values for each reported. Inferential statistics were performed on revision quality. Specifically, the Shapiro-Wilk test was used to assess the data's normality due to the small sample size. The data are considered to follow a normal distribution if the p-values are greater than 0.05 (Thode, 2002). When normality is confirmed, an independent samples t-test will be employed to investigate differences between the two groups; otherwise, a Mann-Whitney U test will be applied. These analyses were conducted using

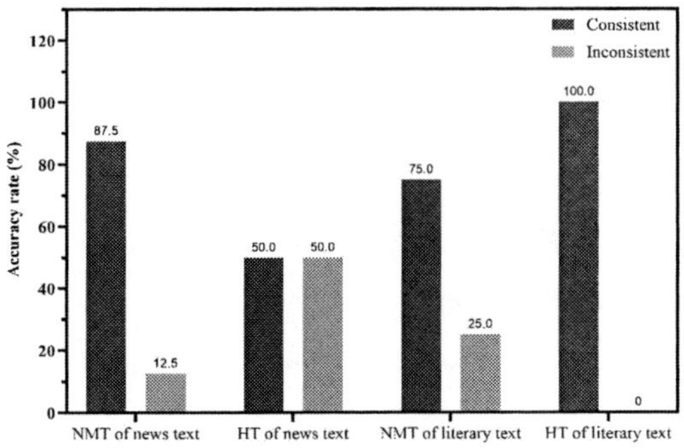

Figure 1: Accuracy rate of participants' perceptions. *Consistent* = perception matches actual source, *Inconsistent* = perception does not match actual source.

SPSS 26.0. Furthermore, GPower 3.1, a tool for statistical power analyses, was used to compute Cohen's d, a widely recognized measure of effect size. An effect size of 0.2, 0.5, or 0.8 corresponds to small, medium, or large effects, respectively (Cohen, 1988). Sawilowsky (2009) further revised the rules of thumb for effect sizes to define 0.01 (very small), 1.2 (very large), and 2.0 (huge).

4 Results

4.1 Accuracy rate of perceived sources of translations

The accuracy rate of participants' perceived sources of translations was examined across four different scenarios: NMT of news text, HT of news text, NMT of literary text, and HT of literary text (see Figure 1). The findings suggest that participants were more accurate in identifying the source of NMT-translated news text compared to human-translated news text. However, the accuracy rate for human-translated literary text is higher than that for NMT-translated literary text. It could be seen that that participants were better at recognizing the source of NMT-translated news text and human-translated literary text.

4.2 Criteria for determining sources of translations

The criteria were investigated via participants' comments across four scenarios in consistent and inconsistent situations. For NMT of news text, 87.5% of participants identified the output as machine-translated based on literal translation strategies. Most participants noted that the translation was 'overly literal' or that the sentence structures 'closely followed the ST, lacking flexibility in segmentation and cohesion.' 50.0% of participants attributed their judgment to a terminology error. For instance, they highlighted the mistranslation of the term'一带一路' ('the Belt and Road Initiative') as 'the Belt and Road', further suggesting NMT involvement. However, 12.5% of participants argued that the translation was produced by a human translator and claimed, 'Since NMT typically ensures terminology accuracy, this terminology error suggests the involvement of a human translator.'

For HT of news text, 50% of participants attributed the translation to a human translator due primarily to free translation strategies, including omission, word class shifts and meaning-based sentence restructuring. For instance, they believed that omission is a strategy commonly employed by human translators to address Chinese parallelism, where the same idea is conveyed through two similar phrases. In this translation, the parallelism '彼此隔绝、闭关锁国' was translated simply as 'isolation', suggesting the involvement of a human translator. Moreover, the term '受益者' ('the beneficiary') was transformed from a noun in Chinese into a verb phrase in English ('benefit from'). Their perception was further reinforced by the division of the third Chinese sentence into two separate English sentences in the translation. However, 50.0% of participants argued the translation was NMT-produced, noting its 'awkward and unnatural flow' or stating that most of the text is 'word-for-word', 'closely mirroring the word order in the ST', and 'failing to convey the progressive meaning.'

For NMT of literary text, 75.0% of participants attributed the output to NMT due to its overly literal translation strategies. For instance, the Chinese phrase '钟表上的秒针一下一下的移动' ('a watch or clock ticking away the seconds') was translated literally as 'the second hand on the clock move one by one.' Other awkward translations, such as 'look at the calendars hanging on the wall that can be torn off one by one,' further reinforced their perception that the translation was NMT-generated. However, 25.0% of participants argued the translation was human-produced. For instance, P16 noted that 'the overly wordy translation of the first three Chinese sentences reflected a human translator's interpretation of the ST.'

For HT of literary text, all participants correctly identified its source, as it featured free translation strategies like improved logical cohesion and omissions. For example, the phrase '再看看墙上挂着的日历' (literally 'and look at the calendars hanging on the wall') was translated as 'likewise, as for the calender on the wall.' Similarly, the translation of '因为时间即生命' (literally 'because time is life') as 'after all, time is life' demonstrated a nuanced understanding of logical flow, an ability often regarded as unique to human translators. Participants also believed that a human translator is better equipped to integrate the original meanings and preserve the style of the ST by employing omission strategy, compared to NMT systems. It was interesting to note that only P01 identified the spelling error 'calender' in the human-translated literary text, a technical error that is common in HT but rare in NMT outputs.

4.3 Revision changes

The average number of revision changes was investigated across four scenarios (see Figure 2). For translation segments with errors, participants made the most necessary changes to NMT of literary text, followed by NMT of news text, HT of news text, and HT of literary text. The average number of underrevisions was similar for HT of news text, NMT of literary text, and HT of literary text, while no underrevisions were observed in NMT of news text. These results suggested participants were most effective at detecting and correcting errors in NMT-translated literary text and least effective in HT-translated literary text.

For error-free translation segments, participants introduced more errors in HT of literary text than in the other three scenarios. Additionally, hyperrevisions were most frequent in HT of news text, followed by NMT of literary text, NMT of news text, and HT of literary text. Participants achieved the most improvements to HT of news text and the fewest to HT of literary text. Overall, participants made many changes to error-free segments across all scenarios, with the highest number of changes occurring in HT of news text.

We further compared the average number of revision changes across four scenarios in consistent and inconsistent situations (see Figure 3). For NMT of news text, participants detected and corrected more errors in inconsistent scenarios than in consistent ones. In contrast, for HT of news text and NMT of literary text, participants made more necessary changes and underrevisions when their perception of the source matched the actual origin. The results suggested that participants tended to detect and correct more errors when they believed the news text was human-translated and when they perceived the literary text as NMT-generated.

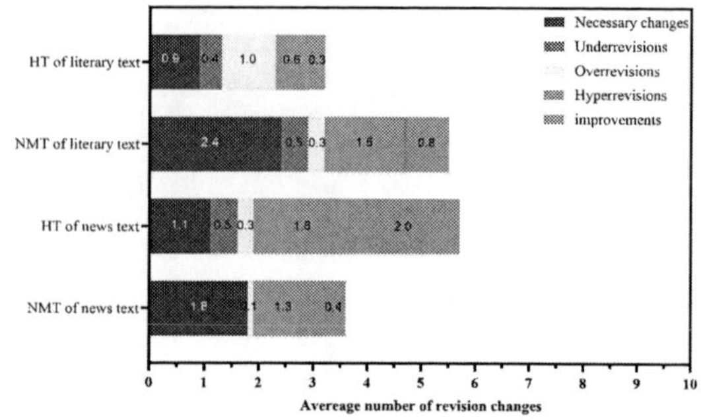

Figure 2: Average number of revision changes across four scenarios

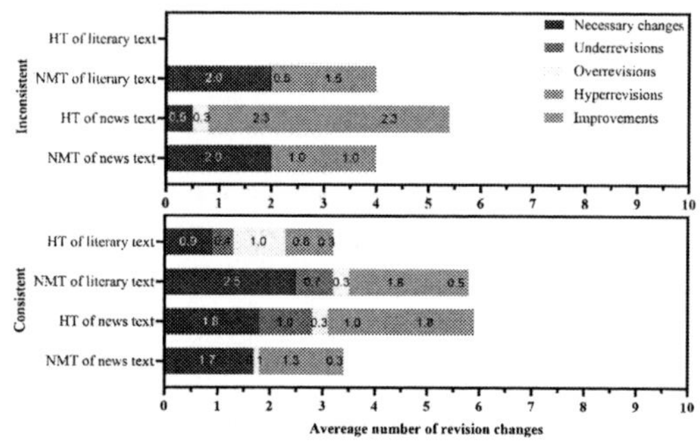

Figure 3: Average number of revision changes across four scenarios in consistent and inconsistent situations

4.4 Revision quality

We first compared the revision quality between the different sources of translation for the same text type. As shown in Figure 4, the revision quality in post-editing NMT of news text ranged from 0.00 to 0.64 (M = 0.21, SD = 0.19), while for revising HT of news text, it ranged from -0.14 to 0.29 (M = 0.12, SD = 0.13). No significant difference in revision quality was found between those two scenarios (t(12.28) = 1.180, p = 0.26, Cohen's d = 0.59). However, post-editing NMT of literary text ranged from 0.14 to 0.57 (M = 0.30, SD = 0.16), while revising HT of literary text ranged from -0.14 to 0.14 (M = 0.01, SD = 0.09). The independent samples t-test showed that the revision quality in post-editing NMT of literary text was significantly higher than that in revising HT of literary text (t(14) = 4.44, p = 0.001 < 0.01, Cohen's d = 2.22).

We also compared the revision quality between different text types within the same translation source. To be specific, post-editing NMT of news text showed lower revision quality than post-editing

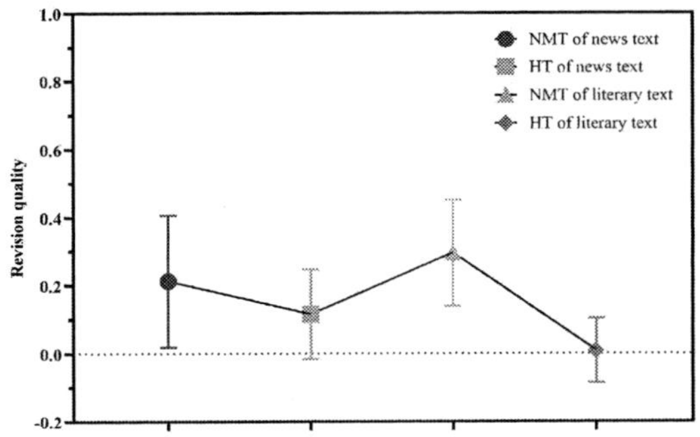

Figure 4: Revision quality in four scenarios

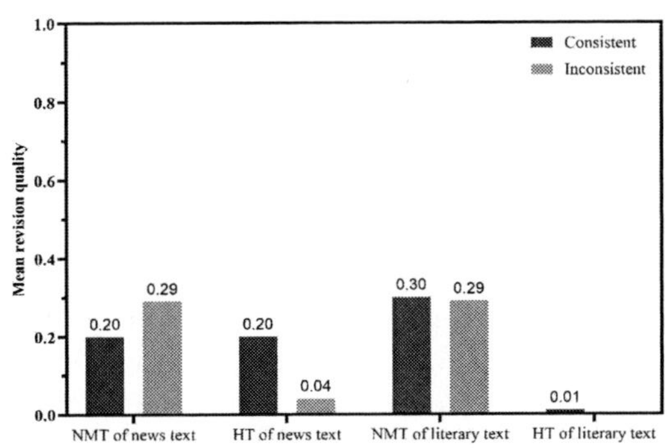

Figure 5: Mean revision quality across four scenarios in consistent and inconsistent situations

NMT of literary text, though the difference was not significant ($t(14) = -0.94$, $p = 0.37$, Cohen's $d = 0.47$). Similarly, revising HT of news text had higher revision quality than revising HT of literary text, but the difference was not significant ($t(14) = 1.86$, $p = 0.09$, Cohen's $d = 0.09$).

Due to the difference in the number of participants between the 'consistent' and 'inconsistent' situations, We only compared the mean revision quality across four scenarios in those two situations (see Figure 5). For post-editing NMT of news text, the revision quality in the consistent situation ($M = 0.20$) was lower compared to the inconsistent one ($M = 0.29$). However, the revision quality of revising HT of news text in the consistent situation ($M = 0.20$) was higher than that in the inconsistent situation ($M = 0.04$). Regarding post-editing NMT of literary text, the revision quality in the consistent situation ($M = 0.30$) was slightly higher than that in the inconsistent ($M = 0.29$). The lowest revision quality score occurred when revising HT of literary text ($M = 0.01$) in cases where participants' perceptions matched the actual source. No inconsistencies were found in HT of literary text.

5 Discussion

5.1 Accuracy rate of perceived sources of translations

This study aimed to investigate the ability of student translators to distinguish between NMT and HT for two distinct text types: news text and literary text. Research on earlier MT paradigms suggests that readers and translators are not always able to reliably distinguish between human and machine translations (He et al., 2010; Vasconcellos and Bostad, 2002). Our findings indicate that participants were quite adept at identifying NMT-translated texts, but for human-translated texts, the type of text appeared to play a significant role.

To be specific, all participants successfully recognized the human-translated literary text, while this was not the case for news text. One plausible reason is that, when translating texts with a higher degree of creativity, human translators can leverage their linguistic competence and personal aesthetic tendency (Chen, 2011) to translate more freely. NMT, however, often struggles with sentence comprehension in literary texts, failing to grasp the underlying semantic connotations (Moneus and Sahari, 2024). As a result, human-translated literary texts are relatively easy to distinguish.

Regarding the difficulty in identifying human-translated news text, it may stem from the nature of news text itself. News text, as a type of informative texts, is embodied by the large amount of terminology in a certain area (Reiss and Rhodes, 2014; Dai and Liu, 2024). Although it is crucial to ensure cultural elements in news texts align with the background of the target audience, information accuracy remains the top priority. Furthermore, Chinese news texts feature clear and concise sentence structures that align with English grammar, meaning that neither human translators nor NMT need to heavily adjust sentence structures when translating into English. Thus, it can be challenging to distinguish between HT and NMT, as both news translations often show similarities in vocabulary and sentence structure.

5.2 Criteria for determining sources of translations

For the criteria for determining the sources of translations, our findings indicated that participants relied heavily on translation strategies and, to a lesser extent, on translation errors. Specifically, participants judging NMT primarily noted literal translation strategies (particularly repetitive sentence structures and disjointed logical flow), as well as terminology errors. Those judging HT, however, reported free translation strategies (including omission, word class shifts, meaning-based sentence restructuring, and adjustments for logical cohesion), and technical errors (such as spelling errors).

Although these two criteria enable most participants to distinguish between NMT and HT, a small group including those who achieved high revision quality were misled by certain misconceptions. First, some believed that NMT systems show remarkable accuracy in terminology, but NMT and other AI technologies may generate mistranslations due to untimely updates to the databases (Zhu et al., 2024) or restrictions for preserving the privacy of sensitive information (Das et al., 2025). This suggests that terminology errors are not exclusive to HT, and terminology translation in NMT deserves particular attention during PE.

Second, NMT systems adopt an 'interpretive' translation strategy, producing overly wordy translations that resemble HT. It might confuse participants with a limited understanding of the differences between NMT and HT, leading them to mistakenly identify such translations as human-translated. These findings are in line with work on student conceptualisations of MT and HT, showing that students do not clearly distinguish between both or understand how MT works (Salmi et al., 2023). It is therefore important to integrate NMT into translator training programs and systematically enhance students' knowledge and critical awareness of both NMT and HT, including their respective strengths, limitations, and suitable application contexts (Li et al., 2025).

5.3 Revision changes

The revision changes to translation segments with errors were analysed first. The findings indicated that participants detected and corrected more errors in NMT than in HT, regardless of text types. A possible explanation is that, although the number of errors and their severity were comparable between NMT and HT in this study, the type of errors might influence participants' revision changes. Critical and accuracy errors are more evident than minor and fluency errors (Carl and Báez, 2019), leading to more opportunities for detection and correction. Thus, participants may have found NMT easier to revise than HT due to its higher frequency of accuracy errors. Moreover, this impact was especially significant in literary texts, as the number of accuracy errors in NMT-translated literary text was twice that in human-translated one.

For revision changes to error-free translation segments, the results revealed that participants were more likely to over-edit segments without errors, especially in NMT-translated literary text and human-translated news text. A possible reason is that the participants did not fully comply with the guidelines for post-editing and revision. These two guidelines required participants to retain as much of the original NMT and HT as possible; however, the results indicated that some participants did not adhere to the guidelines closely. It aligns with earlier observations (Mellinger and Shreve, 2016; Nitzke and Gros, 2020), which suggest that when the original translation conflicts with translators' personal preferences, they may struggle to follow the guidelines and tend to favour their own version, leading to the over-editing of error-free segments. Although most changes to error-free segments do not severely affect the final translation quality, they do increase the cognitive effort and should be avoided (Mossop, 2020).

5.4 Revision quality

As for revision quality, post-editing NMT resulted in higher quality score compared to revising HT, irrespective of text type. This difference in revision quality was significant in the case of literary texts, where participants performed significantly better in post-editing NMT than in revising HT. Given that revision quality is measured by 'necessary changes', 'overrevisions', and 'total translation errors', factors influencing revision changes, such as the types of errors and the translator's adherence to guidelines, may also impact the final revision quality.

An interesting result emerged when comparing revision quality in relation to whether participants' perceived translation sources were consistent with the actual ones. For NMT of news text, the revision quality in the inconsistent situation (revising NMT) was higher than that in the consistent situation (post-editing NMT). In contrast, for HT of news text, the revision quality in the consistent situation (revising HT) was higher than that in the inconsistent situation (post-editing HT). For NMT of literary text, a higher revision quality could be found in the consistent situation (post-editing NMT), compared to the inconsistent situation (revising NMT). The findings are partly in line with the study by Daems and Macken (2020), where the revision quality in two inconsistent situations (revising NMT and post-editing HT) was higher than that in consistent situations (revising HT and post-editing NMT) respectively.

It suggests that the relationship between perception and quality might be mediated by text type. Participants were more likely to achieve higher revision quality not when their perceived translation sources diverged from the actual ones, but when they believed the news text was human-translated and the literary text NMT-generated. It might be attributed to two possible reasons. First, participants might exhibit less tolerance toward HT of news text and NMT of literary text. Their attitude toward HT of news texts is largely influenced by the complex nature of news translation (Yang et al., 2023) and their concerns that the translator's subjectivity might compromise the quality of news translation (Chen, 2011). Their distrust to NMT-translated literary texts may arise from the intricate nature of literary texts (Hu and Li, 2023) and the limitations of current NMT technology (Yu, 2022). However, their sceptical attitudes may foster critical thinking, motivating them to identify and correct errors and ultimately improving revision quality.

Second, this phenomenon can be interpreted through the lens of the Pygmalion Effect (Rosenthal and Jacobson, 1968), which posits that individuals' expectations about the outcome of a task shape their behavioural engagement in it. In HT of news text and NMT of literary text, participants likely held clearer expectations about the desired outcomes and felt more confident in addressing the task. This confidence could motivate them to allocate greater cognitive resources to editing the original translations, driven by their commitment to achieving the anticipated translation quality.

In addition, it is worth noting that the revision quality achieved by participants in this study did not exceed 0.30, lower than that in the study by Daems and Macken (2020). This discrepancy may stem from differences in language pair or translation experience. While Daems and Macken (2020) involved professional translators with rich experience, this study focused on student translators with limited translation experience. Professional translators are typically more adept at employing reading strategies to identify and correct translation errors effectively (Schaeffer et al., 2019), a skill that student translators may lack.

6 Conclusion

This study was conducted to explore student translators' ability to differentiate between NMT and HT across news text and literary text, how they justify their choices, and how they improve the translations. The findings suggest that participants were more adept at identifying NMT-translated news text and human-translated literary text. When determining the translation sources, participants relied heavily on translation strategies and, to a lesser extent, on translation errors. For revision changes, participants detected and corrected more errors in NMT than in HT, regardless of text types, and this difference in error detection and correction between NMT and HT was significant in the case of literary texts. Similarly, participants achieved a higher revision quality in post-editing NMT compared to revising HT, irrespective of text type. This difference in revision quality was significant in the case of literary texts. Furthermore, it was found that participants were more likely to achieve higher revision quality not when their perceptions diverged from the actual translation source, but when they believed the news text was human-translated and perceived the literary text as NMT-generated.

It is also important to note that some limitations should be taken into account when interpreting the findings. To begin with, the small sample size and inadequate sample representation limit the generalization of the findings. The findings of our cross-sectional study reflect students' ability to differentiate between NMT and HT across two text types at a specific point in time. Future studies could, therefore, adopt a longitudinal approach with larger and more diverse samples to track changes in students' ability over time and explore whether translation revision and post-editing practice can effectively enhance their revision and post-editing competence. Second, the text type might have a influence on participants' translation performance, which is worth further investigation.

In conclusion, although this study is exploratory, its findings aim to inspire further research into the potential of NMT for creative texts and the difference between translation revision and post-editing. Such investigations could significantly advance human-computer interaction research in both translation education and the industry.

References

Yuri Bizzoni, Tom S Juzek, Cristina España-Bonet, Koel Dutta Chowdhury, Josef van Genabith, and Elke Teich. 2020. How human is machine translationese? comparing human and machine translations of text and speech. In *Proceedings of the 17th International conference on spoken language translation*, pages 280–290.

Michael Carl and M Cristina Toledo Báez. 2019. Machine translation errors and the translation process: a study across different languages. *The Journal of Specialised Translation*, 31:107–132.

Ya-Mei Chen. 2011. The translator's subjectivity and its constraints in news transediting: A perspective of reception aesthetics. *Meta*, 56(1):119–144.

Jacob Cohen. 1988. Statistical power analysis for the behavioral sciences.

Gloria Corpas Pastor and Laura Noriega-Santiáñez. 2024. Human versus neural machine translation creativity: A study on manipulated mwes in literature. *Information*, 15(9):530.

Ella Creamer. 2024. Dutch publisher to use AI to translate 'limited number of books' into English. *The Guardian*.

Joke Daems. 2022. Dutch literary translators' use and perceived usefulness of technology: the role of awareness and attitude. In *Using technologies for creative-text translation*, pages 53–78. Taylor & Francis.

Joke Daems and Lieve Macken. 2020. Post-editing human translations and revising machine translations. *Translation Revision and Post-editing: Industry Practices and Cognitive Processes*, pages 50–70.

Joke Daems, Sonia Vandepitte, Robert J Hartsuiker, and Lieve Macken. 2017. Translation methods and experience: A comparative analysis of human translation and post-editing with students and professional translators. *Meta*, 62(2):245–270.

Guangrong Dai and Siqi Liu. 2024. Towards predicting post-editing effort with source text readability: An investigation for english-chinese machine translation. *The Journal of Specialised Translation*, (41):206–229.

Badhan Chandra Das, M Hadi Amini, and Yanzhao Wu. 2025. Security and privacy challenges of large language models: A survey. *ACM Computing Surveys*, 57(6):1–39.

Orphée De Clercq, Gert De Sutter, Rudy Loock, Bert Cappelle, and Koen Plevoets. 2021. Uncovering machine translationese using corpus analysis techniques to distinguish between original and machine-translated french. *Translation Quarterly*, (101):21–45.

Félix Do Carmo and Joss Moorkens. 2020. Differentiating editing, post-editing and revision. In *Translation revision and post-editing*, pages 35–49. Routledge.

Sabrina Girletti. 2022. Working with pre-translated texts: Preliminary findings from a survey on post-editing and revision practices in swiss corporate in-house language services. In *Proceedings of the 23rd Annual Conference of the European Association for Machine Translation*, pages 271–280.

Ana Guerberof-Arenas and Antonio Toral. 2022. Creativity in translation: Machine translation as a constraint for literary texts. *Translation Spaces*, 11(2):184–212.

Ana Guerberof-Arenas, Susana Valdez, and Aletta G Dorst. 2024. Does training in post-editing affect creativity? *The Journal of Specialised Translation*, (41):74–97.

James Luke Hadley, Kristiina Taivalkoski-Shilov, Carlos SC Teixeira, and Antonio Toral. 2022. *Using technologies for creative-text translation*. Taylor & Francis.

Hany Hassan, Anthony Aue, Chang Chen, Vishal Chowdhary, Jonathan Clark, Christian Federmann, Xuedong Huang, Marcin Junczys-Dowmunt, William Lewis, Mu Li, et al. 2018. Achieving human parity on automatic chinese to english news translation. *arXiv preprint arXiv:1803.05567*.

Yifan He, Yanjun Ma, Johann Roturier, Andy Way, and Josef van Genabith. 2010. Improving the post-editing experience using translation recommendation: A user study. In *Proceedings of the 9th Conference of the Association for Machine Translation in the Americas: Research Papers*.

Kaibao Hu and Xiaoqian Li. 2023. The creativity and limitations of ai neural machine translation: A corpus-based study of deepl's english-to-chinese translation of shakespeare's plays. *Babel*, 69(4):546–563.

Kristian Tangsgaard Hvelplund. 2011. *Allocation of cognitive resources in translation: An eye-tracking and key-logging study*. Frederiksberg: Copenhagen Business School (CBS).

ISO17100. 2015. Translation services — requirements for translation services.

Arnt Lykke Jakobsen. 2018. Moving translation, revision, and post-editing boundaries. In *Moving boundaries in translation studies*, pages 64–80. Routledge.

Philipp Koehn. 2009. A process study of computer-aided translation. *Machine translation*, 23(4):241–263.

Kalle Konttinen, Leena Salmi, and Maarit Koponen. 2020. Revision and post-editing competences in translator education. In *Translation Revision and Post-Editing*, pages 187–202. Routledge.

Maarit Koponen, Brian Mossop, Isabelle S Robert, and Giovanna Scocchera. 2021. *Translation Revision and Post-Editing*. London: Routledge.

Bernhard Korte and Jens Vygen. 2018. *Combinatorial optimization: theory and algorithms*. Springer.

Hans P Krings. 2001. *Repairing texts: Empirical investigations of machine translation post-editing processes*, volume 5. Kent State University Press.

Ralph Krüger. 2022. Some translation studies informed suggestions for further balancing methodologies for machine translation quality evaluation. *Translation Spaces*, 11(2):213–233.

Samuel Läubli, Sheila Castilho, Graham Neubig, Rico Sennrich, Qinlan Shen, and Antonio Toral. 2020. A set of recommendations for assessing human–machine parity in language translation. *Journal of artificial intelligence research*, 67:653–672.

Xiaoye Li, Xiangling Wang, and Wentian Lai. 2025. The usability of neural machine translation in creative-text post-editing: Evidence from users' performance and perception. *International Journal of Human-Computer Interaction*.

Arle Lommel, Hans Uszkoreit, and Aljoscha Burchardt. 2014. Multidimensional quality metrics (mqm): A framework for declaring and describing translation quality metrics. *Tradumàtica*, (12):0455–463.

Lieve Macken, Bram Vanroy, Luca Desmet, and Arda Tezcan. 2022. Literary translation as a three-stage process: Machine translation, post-editing and revision. In *Proceedings of the 23rd Annual Conference of the European Association for Machine Translation*, pages 101–110. European Association for Machine Translation.

Evgeny Matusov. 2019. The challenges of using neural machine translation for literature. In *Proceedings of the qualities of literary machine translation*, pages 10–19.

Christopher D Mellinger and Gregory M Shreve. 2016. Match evaluation and over-editing in a translation memory environment. In *Reembedding translation process research*, pages 131–148. John Benjamins Publishing Company.

Ahmed Mohammed Moneus and Yousef Sahari. 2024. Artificial intelligence and human translation: A contrastive study based on legal texts. *Heliyon*, 10(6).

Joss Moorkens, Antonio Toral, Sheila Castilho, and Andy Way. 2018. Translators' perceptions of literary post-editing using statistical and neural machine translation. *Translation Spaces*, 7(2):240–262.

Brian Mossop. 2020. *Revising and Editing for Translators*. routledge.

Jean Nitzke and Anne-Kathrin Gros. 2020. Preferential changes in revision and post-editing. In *Translation revision and post-editing*, pages 21–34. Routledge.

Jean Nitzke and Silvia Hansen-Schirra. 2021. *A short guide to post-editing (Volume 16)*. Language Science Press.

Jean Nitzke, Silvia Hansen-Schirra, and Carmen Canfora. 2019. Risk management and post-editing competence. *The Journal of Specialised Translation*, 31(1):239–259.

Daniel Ortiz-Martínez, Jesús González-Rubio, Vicent Alabau, Germán Sanchis-Trilles, and Francisco Casacuberta. 2016. Integrating online and active learning in a computer-assisted translation workbench. *New Directions in Empirical Translation Process Research: Exploring the CRITT TPR-DB*, pages 57–76.

Marta Petrak, Mia Uremović, and Bogdanka Pavelin Lešić. 2022. Fine-grained human evaluation of nmt applied to literary text: case study of a french-to-croatian translation. In *Language Technologies and Digital Humanities Conference*, pages 141–146.

Thierry Poibeau. 2022. On" human parity" and" super human performance" in machine translation evaluation. In *Language Resource and Evaluation Conference*.

Anthony Pym. 2013. Translation skill-sets in a machine-translation age. *Meta*, 58(3):487–503.

Katharina Reiss and Eroll F Rhodes. 2014. *Translation criticism-potentials and limitations: Categories and criteria for translation quality assessment*. Routledge.

Celia Rico Pérez and Enrique Torrejón. 2012. Skills and profile of the new role of the translator as mt post-editor. *Tradumàtica*, (10):0166–178.

Isabelle S Robert, Aline Remael, and Jim JJ Ureel. 2017. Towards a model of translation revision competence. *The Interpreter and Translator Trainer*, 11(1):1–19.

Isabelle S Robert, Iris Schrijver, and Jim J Ureel. 2024. Measuring translation revision competence and post-editing competence in translation trainees: methodological issues. *Perspectives*, 32(2):177–191.

Isabelle S Robert, Iris Schrijver, and Jim JJ Ureel. 2023. Comparing 12 translation, translation revision, and post-editing competences in translation trainees: An exploratory study into dutch–french translation. *Babel*, 69(1):99–128.

Isabelle S Robert, Jim JJ Ureel, Aline Remael, and Ayla Rigouts Terryn. 2018. Conceptualizing translation revision competence: a pilot study on the 'fairness and tolerance'attitudinal component. *Perspectives*, 26(1):2–23.

Robert Rosenthal and Lenore Jacobson. 1968. Pygmalion in the classroom. *The urban review*, 3(1):16–20.

Andrew Rothwell, Andy Way, and Roy Youdale. 2023. *Computer-Assisted Literary Translation*. Taylor & Francis.

Mehmet Şahin and Sabri Gürses. 2019. Would mt kill creativity in literary retranslation? In *Proceedings of the qualities of literary machine translation*, pages 26–34.

Leena Salmi, Aletta G Dorst, Maarit Koponen, and Katinka Zeven. 2023. Do humans translate like machines? students' conceptualisations of human and machine translation. In *Proceedings of the 24th Annual Conference of the European Association for Machine Translation*, pages 295–304.

Shlomo S Sawilowsky. 2009. New effect size rules of thumb. *Journal of modern applied statistical methods*, 8(2):26.

Moritz Schaeffer, Jean Nitzke, Anke Tardel, Katharina Oster, Silke Gutermuth, and Silvia Hansen-Schirra. 2019. Eye-tracking revision processes of translation students and professional translators. *Perspectives*, 27(4):589–603.

Lane Schwartz. 2014. Monolingual post-editing by a domain expert is highly effective for translation triage. In *Proceedings of the 11th Conference of the Association for Machine Translation in the Americas*, pages 34–44.

Giovanna Scocchera. 2020. The competent reviser: A short-term empirical study on revision teaching and revision competence acquisition. *The Interpreter and Translator Trainer*, 14(1):19–37.

Fedor Sizov, Cristina España-Bonet, Josef van Genabith, Roy Xie, and Koel Dutta Chowdhury. 2024. Analysing translation artifacts: A comparative study of llms, nmts, and human translations. In *Proceedings of the Ninth Conference on Machine Translation*, pages 1183–1199.

Arda Tezcan, Joke Daems, and Lieve Macken. 2019. When a 'sport'is a person and other issues for nmt of novels. In *Proceedings of the Qualities of Literary Machine Translation*, pages 40–49.

Henry C. Thode. 2002. *Testing for Normality*. Marcel Dekker.

Antonio Toral and Andy Way. 2018. What level of quality can neural machine translation attain on literary text? *Translation quality assessment: From principles to practice*, pages 263–287.

Eva Vanmassenhove, Dimitar Shterionov, and Matthew Gwilliam. 2021. Machine translationese: Effects of algorithmic bias on linguistic complexity in machine translation. In *16th Conference of the European Chapter of the Associationfor Computational Linguistics, EACL 2021*, pages 2203–2213. Association for Computational Linguistics (ACL).

Eva Vanmassenhove, Dimitar Shterionov, and Andy Way. 2019. Lost in translation: Loss and decay of linguistic richness in machine translation. In *Proceedings of Machine Translation Summit XVII: Research Track*, pages 222–232.

Muriel Vasconcellos and Dale A Bostad. 2002. Machine translation in a high-volume translation environment. In *Computers in Translation*, pages 78–97. Routledge.

Lyu Wang and Xiangling Wang. 2021. Building virtual communities of practice in post-editing training: A mixed-method quasi-experimental study. *The Journal of Specialised Translation*, 36:193–219.

Rebecca Webster, Margot Fonteyne, Arda Tezcan, Lieve Macken, and Joke Daems. 2020. Gutenberg goes neural: Comparing features of dutch human translations with raw neural machine translation outputs in a corpus of english literary classics. In *Informatics*, volume 7, page 32. MDPI.

Yanxia Yang, Runze Liu, Xingmin Qian, and Jiayue Ni. 2023. Performance and perception: machine translation post-editing in chinese-english news translation by novice translators. *Humanities and Social Sciences Communications*, 10(1):1–8.

Yuxiu Yu. 2022. [retracted] english characteristic semantic block processing based on english-chinese machine translation. *Advances in Multimedia*, 2022(1):1458394.

Binghan Zheng, Sandra Báez, Li Su, Xia Xiang, Susanne Weis, Agustín Ibáñez, and Adolfo M García. 2020. Semantic and attentional networks in bilingual processing: fmri connectivity signatures of translation directionality. *Brain and cognition*, 143:105584.

Xiaoqian Zhu, Yanpeng Chang, and Jianping Li. 2024. A cross-institutional database of operational risk external loss events in chinese banking sector 1986–2023. *Scientific Data*, 11(1):939.

A Appendix

		Error types (based on MQM)			Number of errors	Error severity weight		Severity weight of errors
Text type	Translation source	Accuracy	Fluency	Style		Critical	Minor	
News text	HT	1	2	5	8	6	2	14
News text	NMT	2	1	5	8	6	2	14
Literary text	HT	2	0	6	8	6	2	14
Literary text	NMT	4	1	3	8	6	2	14

Figure 6: Error types for each text and translation source

Effects of Domain-adapted Machine Translation on the Machine Translation User Experience of Video Game Translators

Judith Brenner[1], **Julia Othlinghaus-Wulhorst**[2]
[1] University of Eastern Finland
[2] Native Prime
jbrenner@uef.fi

Abstract

In this empirical study we examine three different translation modes with varying involvement of machine translation (MT) post-editing (PE) when translating video game texts. The three modes are translation from scratch without MT, full PE of MT output in a static manner, and flexible PE as a combination of translation from scratch with PE of only those automatically translated sentences deemed useful by the translator. In a mixed-methods approach, quantitative data was generated through keylogging, eyetracking, error annotation, and user experience questionnaires as well as qualitative data through interviews. Results for 12 freelance translators show a negative perception of PE and indicate that translators' user experience is positive when translating from scratch, negative with static PE of generic MT output, and neutral with a positive tendency with flexible PE of domain-adapted MT output.

1 Introduction

Video games are multifarious, and translating them blends software localization, technical translation, literary translation, and multimodal translation (Jimenez-Crespo, 2024). The creative field of video game localization, where the act of translating is only one part of localizing a video game for a target market, is under-researched (Zoraqi and Kafi, 2024). At the time the statistical machine translation (SMT) paradigm was prevalent, consensus in the game localization industry was that machine translation (MT)[1] was not useful for game material. With the shift to neural MT (NMT), this notion changed gradually, following behind the general adoption of NMT in the translation industry (just as it followed behind the adoption of computer-aided translation tools; Moorkens et al., 2024). By now, some game publishers and game localization service providers have adopted processes that include post-editing (PE) of NMT output (Akhulkova, 2021; Anselmi and Rubio, 2020; Lionbridge Games, 2024), the main drivers for PE in game translation being the increase of translation speed and the reduction of translation costs (Moorkens et al., 2024).

Although PE is in demand by game localization buyers (Rivas Ginel and Theroine, 2022), freelance translators who provide the translations needed for game localization push back on this practice. In several manifestos published by game translators personally or together with other media translators represented by professional associations, they argue against the use of machine-generated translations, claiming it dismisses human expertise (En Chair et en Os, 2023) and that PE reduces translation quality (Danilov, 2023), inhibits creativity, and is slower than translation from scratch (Deryagin et al., 2021). Based on these points, the comprehensive Machine Translation Manifesto published by the Audiovisual Translators Europe association argues to consider MT as a tool that contributes to the notion of the augmented translator, where the translator is "front and centre and uses technology to enhance their capabilities" (Deryagin et al., 2021, p. 1).

With contradictory claims about the usefulness of PE in game translation between buyers and providers, our research aims to better understand the PE process when translating video games. By focusing on the video game translator's point of view, we contribute to a shift in MT research

[1] In this article we use "MT" as an umbrella term for all forms of automatic translation, regardless of the underlying technological framework. We specify "SMT" and "NMT" when the technological framework is important for specificity.

Proceedings of the Second Workshop on Creative-text Translation and Technology (CTT), pages 27–43, June 24, 2025

proposed by O'Brien (2023) toward human-centered augmented translation, where one aspect is the impact of translation tools on the experience of their users (Briva-Iglesias et al., 2023).

We conducted a study with video game translators who translated parts of a video game under three different translation conditions with varying involvement of PE. The participants were divided into two groups, where one group used generic NMT, and the other group used domain-adapted NMT. Visiting the translators in their home offices, we observed the translation process over a full day using eyetracking and keylogging and captured the user experience with pre- and post-task questionnaires. The study was conducted in collaboration with the game localization service provider Native Prime. Native Prime supported the research by recruiting the study participants and compensating them for their time spent on the study according to a rate negotiated individually between each participant and Native Prime, by providing the game material to translate, resources such as access to the MT system ModernMT, to the terminology database (TB) and translation memory (TM) for the game translation project, and by setting the project up in the translation management system memoQ TMS. Native Prime is interested in the research results as a basis for their strategic decisions about if and how to offer PE as a service while ensuring a good translator experience. Nonetheless, technical and organizational measures were taken to ensure they cannot directly connect participants to the results.

In this article, we first review the current state of research on PE with professional translators. We then explain the experimental setup, followed by presenting the experiment's results concerning perception of PE and user experience. The results are then discussed in relation to other research findings, leading to some conclusions.

2 Related Work

As no publications appear to exist yet on the use of MT or PE when translating video games – a gap also observed by Hansen and Houlmont (2022) and Zhang (2022) –, we informed our study based on PE research in information-centered fields as well as in creative fields such as literary translation and multimodal fields such as subtitling.

Studies on PE in information-centered fields such as banking and finance or software localization report a general increase in productivity compared to translation from scratch (Läubli et al., 2019; Macken et al., 2020), although this increase does not happen for all translators and has a high variability (Macken et al., 2020; Terribile, 2024). On the contrary, in creative fields such as literary translation, productivity can be noticeably decreased (Guerberof-Arenas and Toral, 2022). Quality of translations in banking and finance seems not to be affected whether or not they were produced by post-editing MT output (Läubli et al., 2019). Yet, a quality analysis of post-edited subtitles for TV series showed inferior quality compared to subtitles translated without PE (Hagström and Pedersen, 2022). Additionally, the level of creativity can be decreased in literary translations produced with PE (Guerberof-Arenas and Toral, 2022). With contradictory results for both productivity and quality between PE studies on information-centric texts and on literary texts and subtitles, the question remains how productivity and quality are affected when PE is involved in translating video games, where informative texts and creative texts merge.

PE productivity relates to the translation process, whereas quality relates to the translation product. For a human-centered take on PE, the effects on the translators are of interest as well. Regarding cognitive effort when post-editing, a study on general texts found PE to be cognitively less demanding for the translators than translation from scratch (Daems, 2016). Also, studies with literary translators found PE to cause less cognitive effort than translating from scratch (Ruffo et al., 2024; Toral et al., 2018). However, when asked about their opinion about post-editing, game translators with a diverse set of backgrounds find it inconvenient and not useful (Rivas Ginel, 2023). A survey among German audio-visual translators revealed that those respondents who are specialized in game translation speak out more negatively against the use of MT in general and the most negative aspect in their opinion is the MT output quality (Jaki et al., 2024). In a study with literary translators that compared PE of SMT and NMT with translation from scratch, participants still preferred translation from scratch, even when they learned that their PE productivity was higher than their translation productivity (Moorkens et al., 2018). Such negative points of views can be better understood by studying the user experience of the translator as user of machine translation (Briva-Iglesias, 2024). As part of a human-centered approach in MT research, Briva-Iglesias (2024) proposes to examine the user experience before and after PE tasks and introduces the concept of machine translation user experience (MTUX), which encompasses usability, satisfaction, and perception both when anticipating to post-edit as well as after the PE task was performed.

Many PE studies involve traditional PE, where entire documents are pretranslated with MT output and consequently everything has to be reviewed and edited (Briva-Iglesias et al., 2023). Some PE studies combine MT output with translation memories (TM) (Macken et al., 2020; Terribile, 2024), where the TM is used to pretranslate sentences with partial TM matches above a certain threshold and the remaining sentences below the threshold are pretranslated using MT. Even fewer studies look at the use of MT for translation support without pretranslation of entire documents (see Vieira 2020 for different ways of employing MT while translating), for example by using adaptive or interactive MT systems where the translator starts typing and the MT system suggests how to complete the sentence (Briva-Iglesias et al., 2023). Some authors propose to study alternatives to PE, such as Hansen and Houlmont (2022) who in the context of game translation propose to use MT not for post-editing but as an additional resource to the TM, in order to not constrain translators' creativity; or Rothwell (2023) who questions the usefulness of pretranslation with MT for literary translation and recommends to explore alternative forms of applying MT in creative text translation.

3 Experimental Setup

The group of interest in our study is professional freelance translators as this is by far the largest group among game translators (Rivas Ginel, 2023; Zoraqi and Kafi, 2024). We decided to employ an experiment in the field because these experiments render results closer to the real working conditions than laboratory-based experiments (Teixeira and O'Brien, 2019). A field experiment also allows us to observe each participant over a longer period, in our case, one full working day. We decided to conduct experiments instead of surveys as we are interested in obtaining measurements from the PE process which are then put into perspective by participant-declared perceptions of it. Lastly, we are interested in comparing a generic NMT system with a domain-adapted NMT system as we want to understand if compiling material for domain adaptation is advisable, considering that game localization poses specific challenges for NMT models (Anselmi and Rubio, 2020; Díaz Montón, 2024), or if PE of NMT can be a viable option for game translation projects where no previous resources for domain adaptation are available.

3.1 Participants

For this study, 15 professional game translators were recruited for four language pairs. They all translate from English into one of the European languages French, Italian, German, or Spanish, the main languages the industry partner provides services for. The participants were recruited from the industry partner's pool of translators and selected based on the following criteria: a) specialization in video game localization, b) language pair, c) place of residence, d) availability, and d) willingness to participate in the study.

The 15 translators gave their consent for participation and data processing in writing. The data generated with their help is kept anonymous from the industry partner. For 2 participants, the experiment sessions could not be completed due to technical problems, so in the end 13 valid data sets could be obtained. Of these 13 participants, 12 were freelance translators with translation being their main occupation and 1 participant with a salaried position in a game localization role and some game translation experience. As the focus of this article is the user experience of professional freelance translators, we remove this participant from the analysis in this article. For one freelancer participant, one of three post-task questionnaires is missing. As this is only a small portion of the entire data set of that participant, and all other data provided by them is of high quality, we contain this participant in the analysis. This results in an even distribution of language pairs, with three freelance participants per target language in the analysis.

The 12 participants under investigation in this article include 6 male and 6 female translators (0 with other gender and 0 prefer not to say), 5 of them between 25 and 34 years, 3 between 35 and 44 years, and 4 between 45 and 54 years of age. The majority is highly educated, with 8 participants holding at least 1 master-level degree in translation or languages, 2 participants with a bachelor's degree in translation, out of which 1 participant has incomplete master's studies, and 2 participants without university education. Their experience working as game translator ranges for 3 participants between 1 and 5 years, for 4 participants between 6 and 10 years, for 2 participants between 11 and 15 years, and for 3 participants between 16 and 20 years. Their work experience translating in other domains ranges from 0 to 30 years. The higher number of years working in other domains suggests a specialization on video game translation occurred over the course of the participants' careers, which is also backed by 10 participants indicating that they mainly or exclusively translate video games, whereas only 2 participants also translate in other domains.

Regarding the participants' experience with PE, 9 participants report prior PE experience. 8 out of these have PE experience when translating games, ranging from 5 months to 2 years. 1 participant has no PE experience in games but 10 months in other domains. 5 participants have PE experience both in games and other domains, and their PE experience in other domains ranges from 1 to 10 years.

3.2 Translation Resources

The aim was to let participants work on a realistic game translation project. We simulated a project where a game that has been translated before gets updated with new content to translate. In such a scenario, typically several resources are available.

The game as object of investigation was chosen by the industry partner. It is a match-3 and hidden-object mobile game revolving around the themes of mysteries and crime-solving. It was picked because it comprises different content types (descriptive text, user interface, dialogs, system messages, etc.) and the translation demands creativity and context sensitivity, while not being too complex. Furthermore, the industry partner had extensive project resources available (comprehensive TMs and a TB in the respective language pairs, reference material for familiarization, etc.).

All participants were provided with a 17-minute gameplay video prepared by the developers of the game for the original localization process. The video served as an introduction to the game so the participants could understand what the game is about and how it is played. In addition, they were presented with 2 pages of localization guidelines from the developers, including information about the game, requested tone and style, formatting specifics, important terminology, and length limitations. The familiarization material was handed to the participants at the beginning of the experiment session to ensure that they all take the time to review it. They could refer to the material anytime during the translation tasks.

Each participant was provided with their own, dedicated memoQ project and anonymized user account with exact same project settings, including a copy of the project's original TM and TB with some adjustments: The TM was cleaned from the segments that were selected for the translation tasks of the study. Moreover, all high fuzzy matches above 90% between the TM and the documents to translate were removed from the TM to make sure the translators had to come up with their own translations by preventing the TM to present a complete translation. As there were no matches between 81% and 89%, this resulted in a TM containing only matches with an 80% match rate or lower. This was relevant for preparing the static PE task. If there had been TM matches between 85% and 89%, we would have used these during the pretranslation step instead of pretranslating entirely with ModernMT. The modified TM included 7,067 segments with a total of around 74,500 words per language. The same TM was also used to create the domain-adapted MT version.

The TB had been created during the original translation of the game by the translators and reviewers in charge of the localization at that time. To make sure that all participants work under the same conditions, the industry partner made sure that the TB contained a similar number of terms in each language. The final TB for the experiment contained 292 terms. The translation documents for the experiment sessions had been prepared in Excel and then imported into each of the memoQ projects with preconfigured settings and filter configurations to make sure all participants worked under the exact same conditions.

ModernMT was included in the memoQ projects in form of an integrated memoQ plugin. According to its website[2], ModernMT is a self-learning MT technology based on neural networks. It was picked for this study because a) it offers document-level adaptation (i.e., it elaborates the translation based on the whole document and not just single sentences), b) it learns from corrections in real time, c) its engine can be further adapted through existing TMs, and d) it can be used with different workflows (static and dynamic).

[2] `https://www.modernmt.com`

Participants had internet access to perform research while translating.

3.3 Translation Tasks

The translation tasks were designed to be as close to a typical game translation job as possible. Each participant translated three documents that were compiled by manually selecting strings from the game. All three documents were structured the same, with a similar number of strings for each content type, such as dialogues, user interface, descriptive texts, and the game's description for an online shop. The documents were between 820 and 850 words long, comprising of 2,496 words in total. All participants translated the same documents, but in different orders (see Table 1).

The participants were tasked to translate under three different conditions: C1 – translation from scratch, C2 – static post-editing, and C3 – flexible post-editing. In C1, translation from scratch, participants worked in a document where at the start all target segments were empty. They had the TB and the TM available as resources, but not MT. In C2, static PE, the entire document was pretranslated with ModernMT. Again, participants had access to the TB and the TM. In C3, flexible PE, the target segments again were empty at the start and participants had the TB and the TM available. Additionally, they also received suggestions from ModernMT. These were generated at the time of activating a segment for translation and shown alongside the TB and TM matches in the Translation Results pane to the right of the target text column in the memoQ translation editor. The pretranslation for C2 was generated on the morning of each participant session to ensure that the ModernMT output quality for C2 would be similar to the ModernMT output quality in C3 on the same day for each participant.

Moreover, participants were divided into two groups, with each group receiving MT suggestions from a different MT version. ModernMT can be either used in its generic state off the shelf (group A), or tuned with a TM, creating a domain-adapted version (group B). For group B, the same TM of around 74,500 words that was also available during translation was added to ModernMT to create a version adapted specifically to the game under translation. During the study, participants did not know which ModernMT version they used.

Conditions as well as documents were rotated among the 15 participants to account for learning and fatigue effects (see Table 1). Participants only had access to their own copy of the TM to ensure they do not see TM entries originating from other participants before them. From one task to the next, each participant used a fresh copy of the TM, meaning they had no access to what they had translated in the previous translation task. This was to make sure that the productivity data for all three tasks remained comparable.

Parti.	Lang.	Task1	Task2	Task3	Group
P01	DE	C1T2	C2T3	C3T1	B
P02	DE	C1T1	C3T3	C2T2	B
P03	DE	C2T1	C1T3	C3T2	A
P04	ES	C1T2	C2T1	C3T3	A
P05	ES	C3T1	C2T2	C1T3	B
P06	ES	C2T3	C1T1	C3T2	A
P07	FR	C1T3	C3T2	C2T1	B
P08	FR	C3T3	C1T1	C2T2	B
P09	FR	C2T3	C3T1	C1T2	A
P10	IT	C3T3	C1T1	C2T2	A
P11	IT	C3T2	C2T1	C1T3	A
P12	IT	C3T1	C1T2	C2T3	B

Table 1: Rotated assignment of conditions (C1, C2, C3), documents (T1, T2, T3), and MT version (group A, B).

Translation took place in memoQ 11.2, a computer-aided translation tool commonly used for game translations (Rivas-Ginel, 2023) and the industry partner's tool of choice.

3.4 Data Generation

Data was generated at the home offices of participating freelance game translators in France, Italy, Germany, and Spain in December 2024 and January 2025. Most of the translators worked at their usual desks, sitting in their usual chairs and were operating their own mice and keyboards. To fulfill the hardware requirements for the eyetracker, a Tobii Pro X3-120, we brought a 22" screen to which the eyetracker was attached, along with the eyetracker's external processing unit (EPU) and a laptop on which the translation tasks were performed. With his setup participants worked in their usual environment instead of in a lab and their data privacy was protected as no software needed to be installed on participants' PCs.

Each participant session lasted for a full working day. A session began with setting up the workstation and ensuring the eyetracker was able to track the participant's eye movements. While the researcher prepared the memoQ project and the eyetracking project for the first task, the participant used the familiarization material to get acquainted with the game project. They could take as much time for this as needed. Then they were introduced to the first task to set expectations, followed by answering the pre-task questionnaire. After the questionnaire, they started with their first translation task of the day. For each task, they were expected to translate the entire document including self-revision to create a translation to the same level of quality they typically deliver to the industry partner. All translators were encouraged to take breaks to counter fatigue effects. They all took short breaks during the translation tasks and longer breaks between the tasks. After each task, they filled in the post-task questionnaire for capturing their user experience. The day was concluded with a short interview, followed by dismantling the workstation and packing the research equipment.

3.5 Measurements

The eyetracker logged the time taken for the translation tasks, the keystrokes and mouse actions, the gaze data such as fixations, and created a screen recording of everything happening on the main screen the participants were working on.

The resulting translations of each task were saved for a subsequent error analysis, which will be reported on in a future publication.

Before the first translation task and after each of the three translation tasks, participants responded to questionnaires. The pre-task questionnaire asked for demographic data, professional experience, their translation process, experience with machine translation and post-editing as well as their perception of MT and PE. We compiled this questionnaire by combining items relevant for our study from the validated Translation and Interpreting Competence Questionnaire (TICQ; Schaeffer et al., 2019), Briva-Iglesias' (2024) pre-task questionnaire, and a questionnaire directed at literary translators about their use of translation technology (Ruokonen and Salmi, 2024).

Immediately after each of the translation tasks, participants responded to a self-reported user experience questionnaire (UEQ; Laugwitz et al., 2008). The UEQ is a validated questionnaire developed to measure the user experience and usability of an interactive software product. In the UEQ, participants use a 7-step scale to indicate their level of agreement with 26 items. The items fall under 6 dimensions that cover aspects such as the overall impression, how easy it is to learn, how efficient the usage is, if the user feels in control, if the usage is exciting and motivating, and if it is innovative and creative (Schrepp et al., 2014). The 26 items represent pairs of adjectives that are extreme opposites to each other, such as "1 annoying – 7 enjoyable". The order in which the 26 items are presented is randomized for each individual post-task questionnaire. Half of the items are presented with the negative adjective on the left of the 7-step scale and the positive adjective on the right, while it is the other way around for the other half of the items. The full list of adjective pairs is available in appendix A. Although the UEQ is available in different language versions, the post-task questionnaires were provided to all study participants in English only. This contributed to language conformity between all questionnaires.

After the translation tasks and the respective questionnaires were completed, participants gave a short interview in which they were asked about their overall impression of the three different tasks, about the types of PE they had done before, whether they would consider using MT if they could choose freely, what needed to improve for MT to be useful in their work, and what potential they saw in large language models and generative AI applications for supporting their work as video game translators. The interviews were conducted in English with all participants. This created equal conditions for all participants as otherwise the German participants might have had an advantage in being interviewed in their native language.

4 Results

Here we report on the perception of PE and the user experience observed in this study. A presentation and discussion of productivity and eyetracking data as well as translation quality is out of scope of this article (see Brenner 2024 and Forthcoming for further analysis plans). Statistics were calculated and tables and figures were generated with jamovi version 2.6.26 and the vijPlots module.

4.1 PE Perception before Translation Tasks

Four items in the pre-task questionnaire were designed to measure the participants' perception of PE. These items were taken from the PE pre-task questionnaire by Briva-Iglesias (2024).

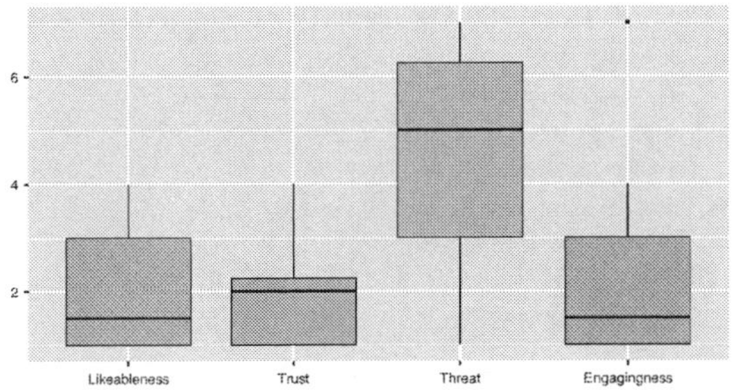

Figure 2: Pre-task perception of PE; n = 12.

The four items were as follows:

a) On a scale of 1–7, where 1 is "Strongly Dislike" and 7 is "Strongly Like", please rate your perception of doing MTPE tasks in professional game translation projects.
b) On a scale of 1–7, where 1 is "Not trustworthy at all" and 7 is "Very trustworthy", please rate if you can trust MTPE to help you successfully deliver a professional game translation project.
c) Please rate how much you agree or disagree with this statement: Machine Translation is a threat to the sustainability of the profession of game translators. (scale 1–7, fully disagree to fully agree)
d) Please rate the following statement: When I am doing MTPE tasks, I find them… (In case you have never done MTPE, answer what you think how you might find it.) (scale 1–7, boring to engaging)

Most participants do not like PE in game translation: Out of 12 participants, 6 assessed this item with the lowest rating of 1, "strongly dislike". No participant gave a higher rating than 4.

The trust in PE to be a good help in game translation is also low, with 9 participants assessing this item with 1 or 2. No participant gave a higher trust rating than 4.

Most participants regard machine translation as a threat to the sustainability of the profession of game translators, with 7 participants assessing this item with 5, 6, or 7. One participant neither agrees nor disagrees, rating this item with 4. The remaining 4 participants do not see a large threat, rating this item with 1, 2, or 3.

With 6 participants giving the lowest possible rating of 1, 2 participants giving a rating of 2, and another 2 participants a rating of 3, most participants find PE boring. One participant finds PE neither boring nor engaging, and only one participant finds this type of translation engaging.

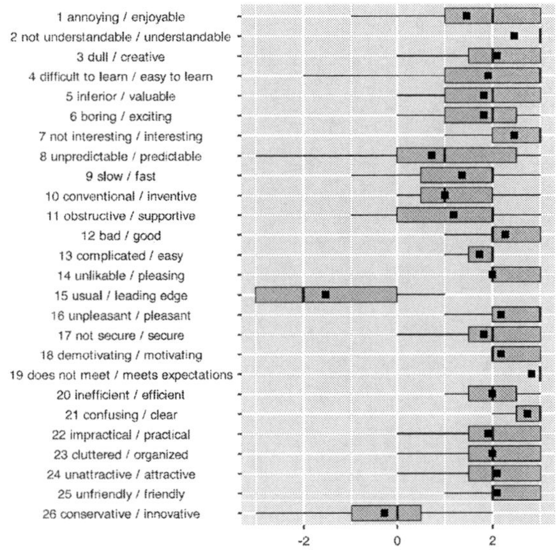

Figure 1: User experience measured after C1 – translation from scratch; n = 11.

Interestingly, this participant had never done PE before becoming a participant in this study. This is also the participant who gave the lowest threat rating. During the interview, it was confirmed that these ratings reflect the participant's opinion.

Figure 2 illustrates the participants' perceptions of PE in game translation as reported at the beginning of the experiment sessions.

4.2 User Experience after Translation Tasks

The UEQ is designed by its original authors with half of the items showing the positive adjective on the left while answering (see appendix A). For analysis, these adjective pairs need to be switched so that all 26 items show the negative adjective on the left. For this, the 7-step scale is converted to a scale from −3 to +3. According to the UEQ authors, all values between −0.8 and +0.8 are interpreted as a neutral experience, whereas values smaller than −0.8 represent a negative experience and values above +0.8 a positive experience (Schrepp, 2023).

4.2.1 User Experience of Translation from Scratch

For the translation condition C1 – translation from scratch, there are 11 post-task questionnaires available for analysis as 1 questionnaire is missing. On average all aspects of user experience when translating from scratch were rated positively, except for "8 unpredictable / predictable", which on average was rated neutral with a mean of 0.73, but a large standard deviation of 2.20. The item "26 conservative / innovative" on average was rated

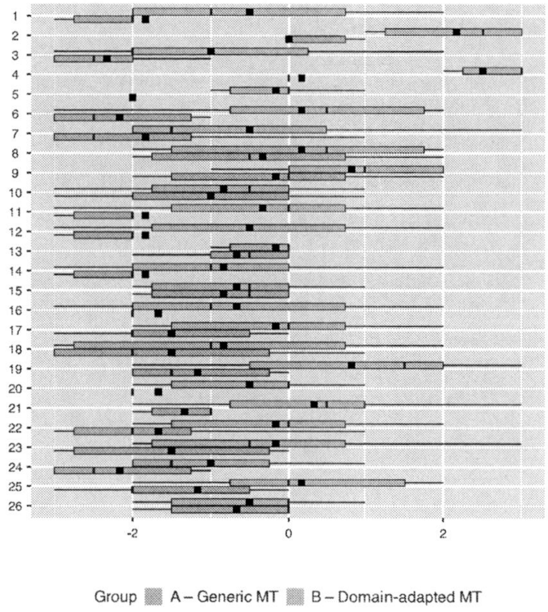

Figure 3: User experience measured after C2 – static PE; n = 12.

neutral as well (M: −0.27; SD: 1.49). The item "15 usual / leading edge" (M: −1.55; SD: 1.57) is the only item with average negative ratings. See Figure 1 for a visualization of all ratings for the user experience of translation from scratch. It clearly shows how almost all aspects were rated on the positive side of the scale.

4.2.2 User Experience of Static PE

For translation condition C2 – static PE, the participants were divided into two groups. Group A (n = 6) used the generic ModernMT output for PE, while group B (n = 6) post-edited the domain-adapted ModernMT output. Figure 3 shows the user experience ratings after task C2 – static PE, with groups A and B side by side for comparison. To save space in Figure 3, items are numbered from 1 to 26. The order of the items is the same as in Figure 1. Appendix A lists the item numbers with their corresponding adjective pairs for reference.

As can be seen in Figure 3, those participants who performed static PE with the generic version of ModernMT (group A) rated the user experience negatively for almost all items (mean, indicated by the black square, below −0.8). Exceptions are items 2 (not understandable / understandable; M: 0.00; SD: 1.67), 4 (difficult to learn / easy to learn; M: 0.17; SD: 0.41), 8 (unpredictable / predictable; M: −0.33; SD: 1.63), 9 (slow / fast; M: −0.17; SD: 1.60), 13 (complicated / easy; M: −0.67; SD: 0.82), and 26 (conservative / innovative; M: −0.67; SD:1.03). With means between −0.8 and +0.8, these 6 items were rated neutral. Based on the mean values, for static PE with generic MT, no user experience aspect was rated positively. Values used in Figure 3 are given in appendix B.

	Group	N	Mean	SD	Minimum	Maximum
11	A – Generic MT	6	-1.83	1.47	-3	1
	B – Domain-adapted MT	6	-0.33	1.86	-3	2
12	A – Generic MT	6	-1.83	1.47	-3	1
	B – Domain-adapted MT	6	-0.50	1.87	-3	2
14	A – Generic MT	6	-1.83	1.47	-3	1
	B – Domain-adapted MT	6	-0.83	1.83	-3	2
16	A – Generic MT	6	-1.67	1.37	-3	1
	B – Domain-adapted MT	6	-0.67	1.97	-3	2

Table 2: Comparison between groups A and B in C2 for items 11 (obstructive / supportive), 12 (bad / good), 14 (unlikable / pleasing), and 16 (unpleasant / pleasant).

Compared to this, group B, who used the domain-adapted version of ModernMT for static PE, rated the user experience more positively for each of the 26 items. The only items rated negatively are items 3 (dull / creative; M: −1.00; SD: 2.00) and 24 (unattractive / attractive; M: −1.00; SD: 1.26), whereas the only items rated positively are items 2 (not understandable / understandable; M: 2.17; SD: 0.98), and 4 (difficult to learn / easy to learn; M: 2.50; SD: 0.84). The remaining 22 items are rated neutral by group B. However, group B shows a wider variance in their user experience ratings compared to group A. This can be most clearly seen in items 11 (obstructive / supportive), 12 (bad / good), 14 (unlikable / pleasing), and 16 (unpleasant / pleasant). Table 2 shows the mean values, the standard deviation, the minimum, and the maximum values for these exemplary items. It is noticeable that the minimum value is −3 for all items, regardless of the group, whereas the maximum value is lower for all items in group A compared to group B. The mean indicates that, on average, group A rated all these items negatively, whereas group B rated them neutral. However, the standard deviation in group B is higher than in group A for all four items.

4.2.3 User Experience of Flexible PE

In translation condition C3 – flexible PE, participants belonged to the same group as in condition C2. Group A (n = 6) received suggestions from the generic ModernMT version, while group B (n = 6) saw the domain-adapted ModernMT

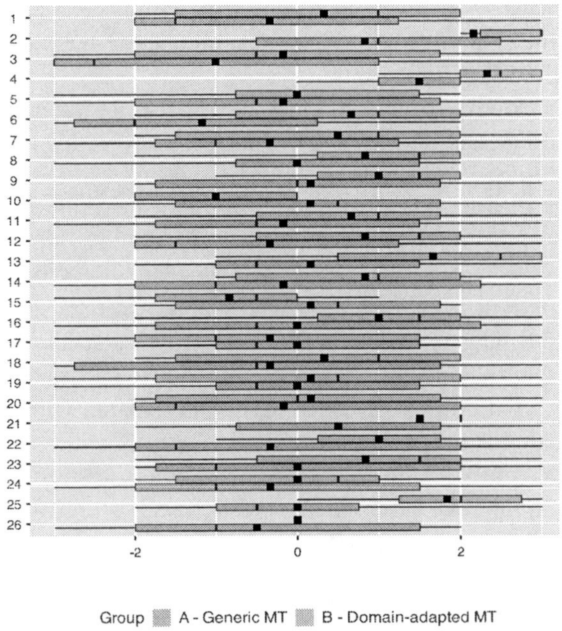

Figure 4: User experience measured after C3 – flexible PE for groups A (n = 6) and B (n = 6).

output. Figure 4 shows the user experience ratings after task C3 – flexible PE, with groups A and B side by side for comparison. Item numbering and ordering is the same as in section 4.2.2.

In C3 (flexible PE), participants who worked with generic MT (group A) rated their experience lower than participants who worked with domain-adapted MT (group B). This matches the same tendency in C2 – static PE. The group difference is especially profound in items 2 (not understandable / understandable), 6 (boring / exciting), 13 (complicated / easy), 22 (impractical / practical), and 25 (unfriendly / friendly), where the differences in mean values between the two groups are larger than 1. Table 3 shows the mean values, the standard deviation, the minimum, and the maximum values for these exemplary items. There are only two items that on average were rated negatively by group B and neutral by group A, item 10 (conventional / inventive; M_A: 0.17; M_B: −1.00) and item 15 (usual / leading edge; M_A: 0.17; M_B: −0.83). However, looking at the standard deviation (item 10: SD_A: 2.32; SD_B: 1.10; item 15: SD_A: 1.83; SD_B: 1.47), we see that the ratings are more varied in group A than in group B.

Overall, in C3 – flexible PE, the ratings are varied within both groups. This can be seen in Figure 4, where for each of the 26 items the horizontal lines reach either the left or the right extreme of the boxplot for at least one of the two groups. Also, the boxes representing the lower and upper quartiles are elongated. Values used in Figure 4 are given in appendix C.

	Group	N	Mean	SD	Minimum	Maximum
2	A - Generic MT	6	0.83	2.04	-2	3
	B - Domain-adapted MT	6	2.17	1.60	-1	3
6	A - Generic MT	6	-1.17	2.14	-3	2
	B - Domain-adapted MT	6	0.67	1.97	-2	3
13	A - Generic MT	6	0.17	1.94	-2	3
	B - Domain-adapted MT	6	1.67	1.75	-1	3
22	A - Generic MT	6	-0.33	2.66	-3	3
	B - Domain-adapted MT	6	1.00	1.41	-1	3
25	A - Generic MT	6	0.00	1.79	-2	3
	B - Domain-adapted MT	6	1.83	1.17	0	3

Table 3: Comparison between groups A and B in C3 for items 2 (not understandable / understandable), 6 (boring / exciting), 13 (complicated / easy), 22 (impractical / practical), and 25 (unfriendly / friendly).

5 Discussion and Conclusion

The PE perception measured at the beginning of the experiment sessions shows that participants do not like PE. They do not trust it being helpful and they find the task of performing PE boring. Most of the participants regard machine translation to be a threat for the sustainability of their profession. This negative view on PE is in line with other studies where participants were asked about their perception of PE. In a survey conducted by Alvarez-Vidal et al. (2020) the satisfaction level with PE was considerably lower than with translation from scratch. In a pre-PE questionnaire used in a study by Ciobanu et al. (2024) less than half of the participants with previous PE experience agreed to liking PE. In a study with literary translators, preference also goes to translation from scratch (Guerberof-Arenas and Toral, 2022).

Briva-Iglesias and O'Brien (2024) point out that "past experiences and perceptions have a great impact and are a determinant for future beliefs, attitudes and behaviours" (p. 445). We see this reflected in our findings in two ways. First, participants in our study, on average, had the most positive user experience with translation from scratch compared to static PE and flexible PE. Translation from scratch is what the highly educated participants have been trained for and what they mostly do in their daily work. Thus, this is the past experience that shapes their user experience while performing the task. Second, we see a negative attitude towards PE uttered before the task reflected in a negative user experience when having done the PE task.

The negative attitude towards PE found in our study is in line with the findings of a survey among game translators world-wide, where the majority of survey respondents finds MT “inconvenient”, “not important”, and “not useful” (Rivas Ginel, 2023, p. 256). The same study also revealed that despite their negative perception, game translators do use MT tools, a finding in line with the results of our pre-task questionnaire.

Measuring the user experience after each of the three translation conditions showed that C1 – translation from scratch is a highly positive experience for all participants. Compared to that, C2 – static PE, the type of PE commonly employed in the translation industry, is a negative experience for those translators who used a generic MT version. For group B, who used the domain-adapted MT version, the user experience of static PE leans more towards neutral, with some translators finding the experience positive. Translation condition C3 – flexible PE is a combination of translation from scratch with PE only of those sentences where the MT output is considered useful by the translator. On average, participants had a better user experience with C3 than with C2. This difference is similar to the results of the MTUX study by Briva-Iglesias et al. (2023), who compared the traditional PE approach (similar to our static PE) with interactive PE, where translators have more control over the use of MT suggestions. In this study, the user experience of interactive PE was significantly higher than that of traditional PE, and the authors attribute this to empowerment and control for the translators.

In our study, user experience was improved when PE was combined with domain-adapted MT, showing that domain adaptation can have benefits for the translators who perform PE. Our results about perception of PE and the MT user experience are mostly in line with studies relating to other domains. In future publications we will analyze the generated data regarding productivity, quality, and translator’s cognitive effort. This will contribute to a wider picture of the PE process when translating video games and potentially show differences to or commonalities with other fields of translation.

6 Limitations

In this study, we simulated a real-world game translation project. As this could only approximate what actually happens when freelance game translators translate and post-edit, there naturally are some limitations.

Study participants were recruited from the pool of freelance translators who have an established business relationship with the industry partner. It was important that an established trust relationship before taking part in the experiment could continue after the experiment. Therefore, candidates with interest in participating who had not worked with the industry partner before could not be considered, limiting the opportunities for anyone to participate.

The limited number of 12 participants with 4 language pairs does not allow a generalization for all video game translators worldwide. Instead, it highlights individual differences between translators that should be considered when assessing PE for video game translation.

As each participant was only exposed to either generic or domain-adapted MT, it might be possible that group A happens to consist of more people with a general negative tendency.

Participants were aware of taking part in an experiment, as the technical setup on their desks was different than usual.

According to Finnish national guidelines for ethical review, a formal ethics review was not required for this type of research (Finnish National Board on Research Integrity TENK, 2019). Still, ethical advisors at the University of Eastern Finland were consulted regarding participants’ remuneration. It was agreed that compensation would not add pressure to participate but, on the contrary, promote research feasibility and quality. During the experiment it was clear that participants treated it like a regular assignment and aspired to deliver their typical quality. Without compensation, it would not have been possible for them to dedicate a full working day to the research.

Acknowledgments

This research was funded by the Finnish Kone Foundation (2023–2025, project number 202202303) and the European Association for Machine Translation (EAMT), Sponsorship of Activities, Students’ Edition 2023, and supported by Native Prime. We wish to thank the 15 study participants for their participation.

References

Yulia Akhulkova. 2021. Machine Translation for Games – An interview with Mikhail Gorbunov.

Sergi Alvarez-Vidal, Antoni Oliver, and Toni Badia. 2020. Post-editing for Professional Translators: Cheer or Fear? *Revista Tradumàtica*(18):49–69. https://doi.org/10.5565/rev/tradumatica.275

Cristina Anselmi and Inés Rubio. 2020. The Future is Here: Neural Machine Translation for Games.

Vicent Briva-Iglesias. 2024. Fostering human-centered, augmented machine translation: Analysing interactive post-editing. Ph.D. thesis, Dublin City University, Dublin, Ireland.

Vicent Briva-Iglesias and Sharon O'Brien. 2024. Pre-task perceptions of MT influence quality and productivity: the importance of better translator-computer interactions and implications for training. In Carolina Scarton, Charlotte Prescott, Chris Bayliss, Chris Oakley, Joanna Wright, Stuart Wrigley, Xingyi Song, Edward Gow-Smith, Rachel Bawden, Víctor M Sánchez-Cartagena, Patrick Cadwell, Ekaterina Lapshinova-Koltunski, Vera Cabarrão, Konstantinos Chatzitheodorou, Mary Nurminen, Diptesh Kanojia, and Helena Moniz, editors, *Proceedings of the 25th Annual Conference of the European Association for Machine Translation (Volume 1)*, pages 444–454, Sheffield, UK. European Association for Machine Translation (EAMT).

Vicent Briva-Iglesias, Sharon O'Brien, and Benjamin R. Cowan. 2023. The impact of traditional and interactive post-editing on Machine Translation User Experience, quality, and productivity. *Translation, Cognition & Behavior*, 6(1):60–86. https://doi.org/10.1075/tcb.00077.bri

Judith Brenner. 2024. The MTxGames Project: Creative Video Games and Machine Translation – Different Post-Editing Methods in the Translation Process. In Carolina Scarton, Charlotte Prescott, Chris Bayliss, Chris Oakley, Joanna Wright, Stuart Wrigley, Xingyi Song, Edward Gow-Smith, Mikel Forcada, and Helena Moniz, editors, *Proceedings of the 25th Annual Conference of the European Association for Machine Translation (Volume 2)*, pages 47–48, Sheffield, UK. European Association for Machine Translation (EAMT).

Judith Brenner. Forthcoming. MTxGames: Machine Translation Post-Editing in Video Game Translation – Findings on User Experience and Preliminary Results on Productivity. Accepted at MT Summit 2025. Geneva, Switzerland.

Dragoş Ciobanu, Miguel Rios, Alina Secară, Justus Brockmann, Raluca-Maria Chereji, and Claudia Wiesinger. 2024. The impact of using text-to-speech (TTS) in post-editing machine translation (PEMT) workflows on translators' cognitive effort, productivity, quality, and perceptions. *Revista Tradumàtica*(22):323–254. https://doi.org/10.5565/rev/tradumatica.394

Joke Daems. 2016. A translation robot for each translator? A comparative study of manual translation and post-editing of machine translations: process, quality and translator attitude. dissertation, Ghent University. Faculty of Arts and Philosophy, Ghent, Belgium.

Lucile Danilov. 2023. Gameloc Manifesto.

Max Deryagin, Miroslav Pošta, and Daniel Landes. 2021. Machine Translation Manifesto. Audiovisual Translators Europe.

Diana Díaz Montón. 2024. Video game localizers. In *Handbook of the Language Industry*, pages 225–250. De Gruyter Mouton, Berlin, Boston. https://doi.org/10.1515/9783110716047-011

En Chair et en Os. 2023. Literature, Film, Press, Video Games: Say No to Soulless Translations.

Finnish National Board on Research Integrity TENK. 2019. The Ethical Principles of Research with Human Participants and Ethical Review in the Human Sciences in Finland. https://tenk.fi/en/ethical-review/ethical-review-human-sciences

Ana Guerberof-Arenas and Antonio Toral. 2022. Creativity in translation: Machine translation as a constraint for literary texts. *Translation Spaces*, 11(2):184–212. https://doi.org/10.1075/ts.21025.gue

Hanna Hagström and Jan Pedersen. 2022. Subtitles in the 2020s: The Influence of Machine Translation. *Journal of Audiovisual Translation*, 5(1):207–225. https://doi.org/10.47476/jat.v5i1.2022.195

Damien Hansen and Pierre-Yves Houlmont. 2022. A Snapshot into the Possibility of Video Game Machine Translation. In Janice Campbell, Stephen Larocca, Jay Marciano, Konstantin Savenkov, and Alex Yanishevsky, editors, *Proceedings of the 15th Biennial Conference of the Association for Machine Translation in the Americas (Volume 2: Users and Providers Track and Government Track)*, pages 257–269, Orlando, USA. Association for Machine Translation in the Americas.

Sylvia Jaki, Maren Bolz, and Sophie Röther. 2024. KI-Technologien in der Audiovisuellen Translation – Umfrageergebnisse aus der deutschen Translationsindustrie. *trans-kom*, 17(2):320–342.

Miguel A. Jimenez-Crespo. 2024. *Localization in Translation*. Routledge. https://doi.org/10.4324/9781003340904

Samuel Läubli, Chantal Amrhein, Patrick Düggelin, Beatriz Gonzalez, Alena Zwahlen, and Martin Volk. 2019. Post-editing Productivity with Neural Machine Translation: An Empirical Assessment of Speed and Quality in the Banking and Finance Domain. In Mikel Forcada, Andy Way, Barry

Haddow, and Rico Sennrich, editors, *Proceedings of Machine Translation Summit XVII: Research Track*, pages 267–272, Dublin, Ireland. European Association for Machine Translation.

Bettina Laugwitz, Theo Held, and Martin Schrepp. 2008. Construction and evaluation of a user experience questionnaire. In Andreas Holzinger, editor, *USAB 2008, Lecture Notes in Computer Science, Vol. 5298*, pages 63–76, Graz, Austria. https://doi.org/10.1007/978-3-540-89350-9_6

Lionbridge Games. 2024. Games Machine Translation Services.

Lieve Macken, Daniel Prou, and Arda Tezcan. 2020. Quantifying the Effect of Machine Translation in a High-Quality Human Translation Production Process. *Informatics*, 7(2). https://doi.org/10.3390/informatics7020012

Carme Mangiron. 2022. Audiovisual translation and multimedia and game localisation. In *The Routledge Handbook of Translation and Methodology*, pages 410–424. Routledge.

Joss Moorkens, Antonio Toral, Sheila Castilho, and Andy Way. 2018. Translators' perceptions of literary post-editing using statistical and neural machine translation. *Translation Spaces*, 7(2):240–262. https://doi.org/10.1075/ts.18014.moo

Joss Moorkens, Andy Way, and Séamus Lankford. 2024. *Automating Translation*. Routledge, London. https://doi.org/10.4324/9781003381280

Sharon O'Brien. 2023. Human-Centered augmented translation: against antagonistic dualisms. *Perspectives*:1–16. https://doi.org/10.1080/0907676X.2023.2247423

María Isabel Rivas Ginel. 2023. *The ergonomics of CAT tools for video game localisation*. PhD thesis, Université Bourgogne Franche-Comté.

María Isabel Rivas Ginel and Sarah Theroine. 2022. Machine Translation and Gender biases in video game localisation: a corpus-based analysis. *Journal of Data Mining & Digital Humanities*, Towards robotic translation? https://doi.org/10.46298/jdmdh.9065

Andrew Rothwell. 2023. Retranslating Proust Using CAT, MT, and Other Tools. In Andrew Rothwell, Andy Way, and Roy Youdale, editors, *Computer-Assisted Literary Translation*, pages 106–125. Routledge, New York. https://doi.org/10.4324/9781003357391

Paola Ruffo, Joke Daems, and Lieve Macken. 2024. Measured and perceived effort: assessing three literary translation workflows. *Revista Tradumàtica*(22):238–257. https://doi.org/10.5565/rev/tradumatica.378

Minna Ruokonen and Leena Salmi. 2024. Finnish literary translators' use of translation technology and tools: processes, profiles, and purposes. *Mikael: Finnish Journal of Translation and Interpreting Studies*, 17(1):138–154. https://doi.org/10.1080/0907676X.2019.1629468

Moritz Schaeffer, David Huepe, Silvia Hansen-Schirra, Sascha Hofmann, Edinson Muñoz, Boris Kogan, Eduar Herrera, Agustín Ibáñez, and Adolfo M. García. 2019. The Translation and Interpreting Competence Questionnaire: an online tool for research on translators and interpreters. *Perspectives*, 28(1):90–108. https://doi.org/10.1080/0907676X.2019.1629468

Martin Schrepp. 2023. User Experience Questionnaire Handbook.

Martin Schrepp, Andreas Hinderks, and Jörg Thomaschewski. 2014. Applying the User Experience Questionnaire (UEQ) in Different Evaluation Scenarios. In *Design, User Experience, and Usability. Theories, Methods, and Tools for Designing the User Experience*, volume 8517, pages 383–392, Cham. Springer. https://doi.org/10.1007/978-3-319-07668-3_37

Carlos S. C. Teixeira and Sharon O'Brien. 2019. Investigating the cognitive ergonomic aspects of translation tools in a workplace setting. In Hanna Risku, Regina Rogl, and Jelena Milosevic, editors, *Translation Practice in the Field: Current research on socio-cognitive processes*, Benjamins Current Topics, pages 79–103. John Benjamins Publishing Company. https://doi.org/10.1075/bct.105.05tei

Silvia Terribile. 2024. Is post-editing really faster than human translation? *Translation Spaces*, 13(2):171–199. Version of Record published: 19 Dec 2023.

Antonio Toral, Martijn Wieling, and Andy Way. 2018. Post-editing Effort of a Novel With Statistical and Neural Machine Translation. *Frontiers in Digital Humanities*, 5(9). https://doi.org/10.3389/fdigh.2018.00009

Lucas Nunes Vieira. 2020. Post-editing of machine translation. In Minako O'Hagan, editor, *The Routledge Handbook of Translation and Technology*, Routledge Handbooks in Translation and Interpreting Studies, pages 319–336. Routledge. https://doi.org/10.4324/9781315311258-22

Xiaochun Zhang. 2022. Video game localization: Translating interactive entertainment. In *The Routledge Handbook of Translation and Media*, pages 369–383. Routledge. https://doi.org/10.4324/9781003221678-27

Amir Arsalan Zoraqi and Mohsen Kafi. 2024. Profiles, Perceptions, and Experiences of Video Game Translators. *Games and Culture*:1–22. https://doi.org/10.1177/1555412023122

A Appendix: Items of the user experience questionnaire

List of the questionnaire items as used for analysis in section 4.2, with the negative adjective on the left and the positive adjective on the right:

1. annoying / enjoyable
2. not understandable / understandable
3. dull / creative
4. difficult to learn / easy to learn
5. inferior / valuable
6. boring / exciting
7. not interesting / interesting
8. unpredictable / predictable
9. slow / fast
10. conventional / inventive
11. obstructive / supportive
12. bad / good
13. complicated / easy
14. unlikable / pleasing
15. usual / leading edge
16. unpleasant / pleasant
17. not secure / secure
18. demotivating / motivating
19. does not meet expectations / meets expectations
20. inefficient / efficient
21. confusing / clear
22. impractical / practical
23. cluttered / organized
24. unattractive / attractive
25. unfriendly / friendly
26. conservative / innovative

List of the questionnaire items as presented while answering the UEQ, where half of the items have the negative adjective on the left and the other half have the negative adjective on the right:

1. annoying / enjoyable
2. not understandable / understandable
3. creative / dull
4. easy to learn / difficult to learn
5. valuable / inferior
6. boring / exciting
7. not interesting / interesting
8. unpredictable / predictable
9. fast / slow
10. inventive / conventional
11. obstructive / supportive
12. good / bad
13. complicated / easy
14. unlikable / pleasing
15. usual / leading edge
16. unpleasant / pleasant
17. secure / not secure
18. motivating / demotivating
19. meets expectations / does not meet expectations
20. inefficient / efficient
21. clear / confusing
22. impractical / practical
23. organized / cluttered
24. attractive / unattractive
25. friendly / unfriendly
26. conservative / innovative

B Appendix: Table with user experience values after C2 – static post-editing

The values in the following table are visualized in the boxplot in Figure 3.

User experience with C2 – static post-editing

	Group	Mean	Median	SD	Min.	Max.
1 annoying / enjoyable	**A**	-1.83	-2.00	1.47	-3	1
	B	-0.50	-1.00	1.76	-2	2
2 not understandable / understandable	**A**	0.00	0.00	1.67	-3	2
	B	2.17	2.50	0.98	1	3
3 dull / creative	**A**	-2.33	-2.50	0.82	-3	-1
	B	-1.00	-2.00	2.00	-3	2
4 difficult to learn / easy to learn	**A**	0.17	0.00	0.41	0	1
	B	2.50	3.00	0.84	1	3
5 inferior / valuable	**A**	-2.00	-2.00	0.63	-3	-1
	B	-0.17	0.00	0.75	-1	1
6 boring / exciting	**A**	-2.17	-2.50	0.98	-3	-1
	B	0.17	0.50	1.94	-3	2
7 not interesting / interesting	**A**	-1.83	-2.50	1.60	-3	1
	B	-0.50	-1.50	2.07	-2	3
8 unpredictable / predictable	**A**	-0.33	-0.50	1.63	-2	2
	B	0.17	0.50	1.83	-2	2
9 slow / fast	**A**	-0.17	0.00	1.60	-2	2
	B	0.83	1.00	1.33	-1	2
10 conventional / inventive	**A**	-1.00	-1.00	1.55	-3	1
	B	-0.83	-0.50	1.47	-3	1
11 obstructive / supportive	**A**	-1.83	-2.00	1.47	-3	1
	B	-0.33	0.00	1.86	-3	2
12 bad / good	**A**	-1.83	-2.00	1.47	-3	1
	B	-0.50	-0.50	1.87	-3	2
13 complicated / easy	**A**	-0.67	-0.50	0.82	-2	0
	B	-0.17	0.00	1.33	-2	2
14 unlikable / pleasing	**A**	-1.83	-2.00	1.47	-3	1
	B	-0.83	-1.00	1.83	-3	2
15 usual / leading edge	**A**	-0.83	-0.50	0.98	-2	0
	B	-0.67	-0.50	1.21	-2	1

User experience with C2 – static post-editing

	Group	Mean	Median	SD	Min.	Max.
16 unpleasant / pleasant	**A**	-1.67	-2.00	1.37	-3	1
	B	-0.67	-1.00	1.97	-3	2
17 not secure / secure	**A**	-1.50	-2.00	1.22	-3	0
	B	-0.17	0.00	1.60	-2	2
18 demotivating / motivating	**A**	-1.50	-2.00	1.76	-3	1
	B	-0.83	-1.00	2.14	-3	2
19 does not meet expectations / meets expectations	**A**	-1.17	-1.50	0.98	-2	0
	B	0.83	1.50	1.94	-2	3
20 inefficient / efficient	**A**	-1.67	-2.00	1.37	-3	1
	B	-0.50	0.00	1.22	-2	1
21 confusing / clear	**A**	-1.33	-1.00	0.52	-2	-1
	B	0.33	0.50	1.75	-2	3
22 impractical / practical	**A**	-1.67	-2.00	1.51	-3	1
	B	-0.17	0.00	1.60	-2	2
23 cluttered / organized	**A**	-1.50	-1.50	1.38	-3	0
	B	-0.17	-0.50	1.94	-2	3
24 unattractive / attractive	**A**	-2.17	-2.50	0.98	-3	-1
	B	-1.00	-1.50	1.26	-2	1
25 unfriendly / friendly	**A**	-1.17	-2.00	1.83	-3	2
	B	0.17	0.00	1.60	-2	2
26 conservative / innovative	**A**	-0.67	0.00	1.03	-2	0
	B	-0.50	0.00	1.22	-2	1

C Appendix: Table with user experience values after C3 – flexible post-editing

The values in the following table are visualized in the boxplot in Figure 4.

User experience with C3 – flexible post-editing

	Group	Mean	Median	SD	Min.	Max.
1 annoying / enjoyable	**A**	-0.33	-1.50	2.25	-2	3
	B	0.33	1.00	1.97	-2	2
2 not understandable / understandable	**A**	0.83	1.00	2.04	-2	3
	B	2.17	3.00	1.60	-1	3
3 dull / creative	**A**	-1.00	-2.50	2.76	-3	3
	B	-0.17	-0.50	2.48	-3	3
4 difficult to learn / easy to learn	**A**	1.50	1.50	1.05	0	3
	B	2.33	2.50	0.82	1	3
5 inferior / valuable	**A**	-0.17	-0.50	2.48	-3	3
	B	0.00	0.00	1.90	-3	2
6 boring / exciting	**A**	-1.17	-2.00	2.14	-3	2
	B	0.67	1.00	1.97	-2	3
7 not interesting / interesting	**A**	-0.33	-1.00	2.34	-3	3
	B	0.50	1.00	2.17	-2	3
8 unpredictable / predictable	**A**	0.00	0.00	1.90	-3	2
	B	0.83	1.50	1.60	-2	2
9 slow / fast	**A**	0.17	0.00	2.14	-2	3
	B	1.00	1.50	1.26	-1	2
10 conventional / inventive	**A**	0.17	0.50	2.32	-3	3
	B	-1.00	-1.00	1.10	-2	0
11 obstructive / supportive	**A**	-0.17	-0.50	2.32	-3	3
	B	0.67	1.00	1.86	-2	3
12 bad / good	**A**	-0.33	-1.50	2.25	-2	3
	B	0.83	1.50	1.94	-2	3
13 complicated / easy	**A**	0.17	-0.50	1.94	-2	3
	B	1.67	2.50	1.75	-1	3
14 unlikable / pleasing	**A**	-0.17	-1.00	2.64	-3	3
	B	0.83	1.00	1.72	-1	3
15 usual / leading edge	**A**	0.17	0.50	1.83	-2	2
	B	-0.83	-0.50	1.47	-3	1

User experience with C3 – flexible post-editing

	Group	Mean	Median	SD	Min.	Max.
16 unpleasant / pleasant	**A**	0.00	-0.50	2.53	-3	3
	B	1.00	1.50	1.79	-2	3
17 not secure / secure	**A**	0.00	-0.50	1.67	-2	2
	B	-0.33	-1.00	2.42	-3	3
18 demotivating / motivating	**A**	-0.33	-0.50	2.66	-3	3
	B	0.33	1.00	1.97	-2	2
19 does not meet expectations / meets expectations	**A**	0.00	-0.50	2.19	-3	3
	B	0.17	0.50	2.48	-3	3
20 inefficient / efficient	**A**	-0.17	-1.50	2.48	-2	3
	B	0.17	0.00	2.14	-2	3
21 confusing / clear	**A**	0.50	0.50	1.87	-2	3
	B	1.50	2.00	1.76	-2	3
22 impractical / practical	**A**	-0.33	-1.50	2.66	-3	3
	B	1.00	1.00	1.41	-1	3
23 cluttered / organized	**A**	0.00	-1.00	2.37	-2	3
	B	0.83	1.50	1.94	-2	3
24 unattractive / attractive	**A**	-0.33	-1.00	2.42	-3	3
	B	0.00	0.50	1.67	-2	2
25 unfriendly / friendly	**A**	0.00	-0.50	1.79	-2	3
	B	1.83	2.00	1.17	0	3
26 conservative / innovative	**A**	-0.50	-1.00	2.17	-3	2
	B	0.00	0.00	0.63	-1	1

Fine-tuning and evaluation of NMT models for literary texts using RomCro v.2.0

Bojana Mikelenić
Faculty of Humanities and Social Sciences, University of Zagreb
bmikelen@ffzg.unizg.hr

Antoni Oliver
Universitat Oberta de Catalunya
aoliverg@uoc.edu

Sergi Àlvarez Vidal
Universitat Autònoma de Barcelona
sergi.alvarez@uab.cat

Abstract

This paper explores the fine-tuning and evaluation of neural machine translation (NMT) models for literary texts using RomCro v.2.0, an expanded multilingual and multidirectional parallel corpus. RomCro v.2.0 is based on RomCro v.1.0, but includes additional literary works in five Romance languages (Spanish, French, Italian, Portuguese, Romanian) and Croatian, as well as texts in Catalan, making it a valuable resource for improving MT in underrepresented language pairs. Given the challenges of literary translation, where style, narrative voice, and cultural nuances must be preserved, fine-tuning on high-quality domain-specific data is essential for enhancing MT performance.

We fine-tune existing NMT models with RomCro v.2.0 and evaluate their performance for six different language combinations using automatic metrics and for Spanish-Croatian and French-Catalan using manual evaluation. Results indicate that fine-tuned models outperform general-purpose systems, achieving greater fluency and stylistic coherence. These findings support the effectiveness of corpus-driven fine-tuning for literary translation and highlight the importance of curated high-quality corpora.

1 Introduction

Parallel multilingual corpora play a crucial role in linguistic research and computational applications, serving as foundational resources for a broad range of disciplines. In linguistics, they enable contrastive studies, lexicographic analysis, and phraseology research (Lefer, 2021), offering insights into language structures and translation patterns across multiple languages. In translation studies, they are used to examine translation strategies, detect shifts in meaning, and provide empirical evidence for translation universals. Beyond theoretical applications, parallel corpora are also essential in translation training (López Rodríguez, 2016), providing students and professionals with real-world examples of translated texts that reflect both linguistic variation and different approaches to translation. Additionally, they are widely used in computational linguistics, particularly in training and evaluating machine translation (MT) systems (Koehn et al., 2007; Koehn, 2020), as well as in terminology extraction (Lefever et al., 2009) and multilingual information retrieval.

Since the effectiveness of MT models largely depends on the quality and quantity of their training data, access to well-aligned, diverse, and representative parallel corpora is crucial for improving translation performance. While large-scale datasets exist for widely spoken languages, there remains a significant gap in high-quality parallel data for specific language pairs, especially when literary texts are involved. Unlike technical or legal texts, which are often characterized by terminological consistency and rigid syntactic structures, literary texts pose unique challenges due to their stylistic complexity, cultural nuances, and need for creativity (Guerberof-Arenas and Toral, 2022). Standard MT models trained on general-purpose corpora struggle to capture these intricacies, often producing translations that fail to preserve the author's style, narrative voice, and the overall reading experience.

Given these challenges, the development of high-quality parallel corpora specifically designed for literary translation is essential for advancing MT capabilities in this domain. This paper describes one such use of an updated and improved version of the RomCro corpus, a multilingual and multidirectional parallel corpus of contemporary literary texts in Romance languages and Croatian. This 2.0 version includes more translation units and another

Proceedings of the Second Workshop on Creative-text Translation and Technology (CTT), pages 44–51, June 24, 2025

Category	RomCro v.1.0	RomCro v.2.0	Difference
Languages	6	7	1
Translation units (TU)	142,470	166,742	24,272
Original texts	27	33	6
Total texts	159	213	54
Millions of words (Mw)	15.7	19.4	3.7

Table 1: Comparison of RomCro v.1.0 and v.2.0

language, Catalan. We have used this improved RomCro corpus to fine-tune different MT models, and conducted automatic evaluations on six language combinations, as well as manual evaluations for Spanish-Croatian and French-Catalan language pairs.

2 Previous work

Despite significant advances in NMT, the automatic translation of literary texts remains one of the most challenging areas of MT research. Unlike technical or legal translation, which prioritizes accuracy and consistency, literary translation must preserve elements such as narrative voice, rhythm, metaphorical expressions, and stylistic nuances. Existing studies have shown that standard NMT systems struggle with these aspects, often failing to reproduce the richness and depth of the original text (Toral and Way, 2015).

Recent research has explored fine-tuning NMT models specifically for literary texts. Hansen and Esperanza-Rodier (2022) investigated the impact of customizing MT systems for fiction translation, demonstrating that fine-tuned models trained on smaller, high-quality datasets perform significantly better than general-purpose NMT systems. However, their study also found that even with domain adaptation, the output still required substantial human post-editing to correct stylistic inconsistencies and ensure readability. Similarly, Oliver (2023) proposed training author-specific NMT models, where an MT system is fine-tuned exclusively on the works of a single writer. This approach has shown promise in maintaining stylistic consistency, although it is highly dependent on the availability of sufficient bilingual training data. Toral et al. (2023) investigate whether it is worthwhile to build a customized MT system trained with a large quantity of in-domain training data (novels) compared to a generic MT system for a fairly well-resourced language pair, English-to-Dutch. A multidimensional evaluation shows that a literary-adapted system performs slightly better. Following the promising results shown in previous research, we use RomCro to fine-tune MT models as well as assess the quality of the resulting translations.

3 RomCro: A Multilingual Parallel Corpus of Literary Texts

RomCro is a multilingual and multidirectional parallel corpus of contemporary literary texts[1] in Romance languages and Croatian. Its first version, RomCro v.1.0 (Bikić-Carić et al., 2023), contains works in six languages: Spanish, French, Italian, Portuguese, Romanian, and Croatian. With 27 original titles and their translations, 142,470 translation units, and 15.7 million words, it stands out for its focus on high-quality literary data and multidirectional alignment, allowing each language to serve as both source and target.

The building of RomCro v.1.0 consisted of several stages, from the selection and the collection of texts, their digitization, segmentation, and alignment, with manual corrections to ensure accuracy. Regarding the selection criteria, novels were prioritized and the availability of translations in all six languages dictated the choices. At the end, out of the possible 162 texts (27 originals and their translations into the remaining five languages), all but three were obtained, making it a well-balanced corpus in terms of language distribution. The corpus is accessible in untagged TMX and TSV documents via the European Language Resource Coordination (ELRC) platform.[2] Annotations contain metadata on original language, author, and title, with segments scrambled to protect copyright.[3]

[1]Out of the 27 originals, 17 were published for the first time in this century. Titles first published in the previous century include one work from the 1910s, two from the 1930s, one from the 1950s, three from the 1980s, and three from the 1990s.

[2]`https://elrc-share.eu/repository/search/?q=romcro`. This is an earlier version of the corpus containing 157 texts, in other words, missing two additional texts.

[3]For a further discussion about copyright issues and how they were dealt with, see Bikić-Carić et al. (2023).

Recent efforts to expand the corpus have introduced three new titles in the languages with the fewest original works in version 1.0: two in Portuguese and one in Croatian, as well as a new language: Catalan. The latter task was carried out in two phases: the first involved incorporating existing translations into Catalan,[4] while the second added three Catalan novels along with their translations into the six existing languages. Out of now 30 titles (27 from the v.1.0 and three new additions), 17 are available in Catalan, and the three Catalan originals have been obtained in all the remaining languages, resulting in a total of 54 texts added to the corpus.[5] This not only broadens the scope of the corpus but also addresses the scarcity of literary parallel corpora for Catalan. Table 1 shows a comparison of the two versions, namely the augmentation by more than 24,000 translation units and 3.7 million words. The updated version, RomCro v.2.0, is available in Sketch Engine (Kilgarriff et al., 2014), while the untagged TSV and TMX are hosted in the HR-CLARIN repository,[6] ensuring its availability for broader linguistic and computational research.[7]

4 Training and Evaluating NMT Systems Using RomCro

In a prior study (Mikelenić and Oliver, 2024), we explored the use of this corpus in training NMT systems tailored to literature, and we summarize the design and results of this first experiment in the next subsection. Building on this foundation, we proceed to describe the current experiment.

4.1 The first experiment: combining RomCro with large parallel corpora

RomCro's potential in training NMT systems tailored to literary texts was demonstrated in Mikelenić and Oliver (2024), where the experiment was completed for five language pairs: from Spanish into French, Italian, Portuguese, Romanian, and Croatian. Five baseline and five tailored to literature systems (using the literary data from RomCro) were trained from scratch in the following manner. RomCro v.1.0 was combined with larger, freely available parallel corpora, such as CCMatrix (sch) and MultiCCAligned (El-Kishky et al., 2020), to create a sufficiently large training dataset. These large corpora were rescored using a confidence-based filtering tool and, for most language pairs, a subset of the rescored data most similar to RomCro was selected to enhance relevance. The training process used Marian (Junczys-Dowmunt et al., 2018) to train general (or baseline) and tailored to literature systems for all five language pairs. Standard metrics, including BLEU (Papineni et al., 2002), chrF2 (Popović, 2015), and TER (Snover et al., 2006), were used to compare the tailored systems with baseline models and Google Translate.

Results showed that the tailored systems outperformed the generic Marian systems and achieved comparable or superior results to Google Translate. However, the Spanish-Croatian system underperformed, probably due to limited training data. Building on these findings, we have used RomCro v.2.0 for the new experiment described in the following subsection.

4.2 Fine-tuning existing models using RomCro

In the current experiment, we were interested in: improving the results for the language pair Spanish-Croatian, making use of RomCro v.2.0 to begin training and evaluating systems for Catalan, and adding human evaluation. We opted for the following language pairs in both directions: Spanish↔Croatian (es↔hr), French↔Croatian (fr↔hr) for control, and French↔Catalan (fr↔ca). The third pair was chosen considering that the results might be more insightful compared to combining Catalan with Spanish, given their similarity and the already demonstrated strong performance of this pair in similar tasks. Since the first experiment where corpora were trained from scratch was not very successful for Spanish-Croatian, and not

[4] This first phase was presented as a poster at the CLARIN Annual Conference 2024, with an extended abstract is available in the Conference Proceedings: https://www.clarin.eu/sites/default/files/CLARIN2024_ConferenceProceedings_final.pdf .

[5] The new titles in Portuguese and Croatian are: Lídia Jorge – *O vale da paixão* (in 6 languages, with Catalan missing), Afonso Cruz – *Os livros que devoraram o meu pai* (in 6 languages, with Romanian missing) and Miroslav Krleža – *Povratak Filipa Latinovicza* (in 5 languages, with Portuguese and Catalan missing). The originals in Catalan are: Jaume Cabré – *Les veus del Pamano*, Albert Sánchez Piñol – *La pell freda* and Mercè Rodoreda – *La Plaça del Diamant*.

[6] https://repository.clarin.hr/items/fe77001c-0e97-4b58-8031-505bfaa45352

[7] This paper centers on the application of RomCro v.2.0 in MT, and therefore presents only an overview of the corpus, limited to aspects we considered important for the task at hand and the objectives of this study. We will detail the building of RomCro v.2.0 in a separate paper.

enough Croatian data was added to change that, we opted for fine-tuning the existing models instead. To keep the experiment consistent, the same was done for the language pair not including Croatian, French↔Catalan.

4.2.1 Training

The training was completed by fine-tuning the Opus-MT models[8] and the multilingual NLLB200 600M distilled model (No Language Left Behind)[9] with RomCro v.2.0. To perform the fine-tuning, we have used the algorithms published by the MTUOC project[10]. We have split the RomCro corpus for each language pair into validation (5,000 segments), evaluation (1,000 segments) and the remaining segments for training.

4.2.2 Automatic evaluation

In Table 2, we present the evaluation results for all the reference and fine-tuned models using three automatic metrics implemented in Sacrebleu[11] (Post, 2018): BLEU, chrF2, and TER. The appendices provide the metric signatures, detailing the exact configuration parameters as reported by Sacrebleu. The best results are highlighted in bold in the table. If multiple results are highlighted, it indicates that the differences are not statistically significant. The OpusMT model has been used as the baseline for comparison.

The conclusions we can draw from the table are that the fine-tuned (FT) models, OpusMT-FT and NLLB200-distilled-600M-FT, outperform the base models while, compared to each other, they perform very similarly overall. For Spanish-Croatian, OpusMT-FT achieves the best results across all metrics, with statistically significant differences observed for BLEU and TER, but not for chrF2. For the Croatian-Spanish pair, some metrics favor OpusMT-FT while others favor NLLB-FT, though none of these differences are statistically significant. In the case of French-Croatian, OpusMT-FT performs better across all metrics, but the difference in chrF2 is not statistically significant. Similarly, for Croatian-French, OpusMT-FT outperforms NLLB-FT in all metrics, except for chrF2, where they perform the same. Conversely, for French↔Catalan, NLLB-FT outperforms OpusMT-FT, though the difference in TER is not statistically significant.

4.2.3 Human evaluation

In addition to automatic evaluations, and to obtain a better insight into the results produced by the MT models fine-tuned with the new corpus, we conducted a human evaluation for the Spanish-Croatian and French-Catalan language pairs. For each language pair, we selected 100 randomized segments, with a number of words between 8 and 25. These short segments were extracted from the test set and typically consisted of a single sentence. Although we acknowledge that sentence-level evaluation has limitations, particularly in domains where discourse-level context is important, we considered it appropriate for a preliminary comparison between model outputs. Future work will incorporate context-aware evaluation over longer spans of text.

We selected, for each language pair, the fine-tuned model that achieved the best performance in the automatic evaluation and compared its output against that of the corresponding baseline model. Specifically, we compared the outputs of the OpusMT and fine-tuned OpusMT models for Spanish–Croatian, and the NLLB-DIST-600M and its fine-tuned variant for French–Catalan.

Two experienced linguists, both native speakers of the target language and with professional experience in translation and post-editing, carried out the human evaluation. The evaluators were not informed of which model had produced which output (i.e., the identity of the MT engine was hidden to ensure blind evaluation). For each segment pair, they were asked to assess which of the two outputs represented a better translation, based on adequacy and fluency. When neither translation was clearly better, they were allowed to mark the pair as "equally good."

The evaluation followed a binary preference protocol: each annotator independently selected the better of the two translations (or marked them as equal), without assigning quality scores. Disagreements, which occurred in approximately 10% of the segments, were resolved through discussion in a follow-up meeting. No formal inter-annotator agreement score was calculated, though agreement was high in both language pairs.

As shown in Table 3, for both language pairs, the fine-tuned models produced a higher number of preferred translations. In two cases, both out-

[8] https://github.com/Helsinki-NLP/Opus-MT
[9] https://ai.meta.com/research/no-language-left-behind/es-es/
[10] https://github.com/mtuoc/MTUOC-finetune-OpusMT and https://github.com/mtuoc/MTUOC-finetune-NLLB
[11] https://github.com/mjpost/sacrebleu

System	BLEU (μ ± 95% CI)	chrF2 (μ ± 95% CI)	TER (μ ± 95% CI)
Spanish-Croatian			
Baseline: OpusMT	16.6 (16.6 ± 1.1)	43.5 (43.5 ± 1.3)	71.1 (71.1 ± 1.4)
OpusMT-FT	**22.0 (21.9 ± 1.3) (p = 0.0010)***	**49.1 (49.1 ± 1.4) (p = 0.0010)***	**65.4 (65.4 ± 1.6) (p = 0.0010)***
NLLB-dist-600M	14.6 (14.6 ± 1.3) (p = 0.0020)*	42.9 (42.9 ± 1.1) (p = 0.0689)	76.5 (76.4 ± 4.7) (p = 0.0190)*
NLLB-dist-600M-FT	20.4 (20.3 ± 1.2) (p = 0.0010)*	48.2 (48.2 ± 1.2) (p = 0.0010)*	67.0 (67.0 ± 1.4) (p = 0.0010)*
eval.es-GoogleT.hr	20.6 (20.6 ± 1.1) (p = 0.0010)*	48.9 (48.9 ± 1.0) (p = 0.0010)*	67.2 (67.2 ± 1.3) (p = 0.0010)*
Croatian-Spanish			
Baseline: OpusMT	22.9 (22.9 ± 1.2)	48.3 (48.3 ± 1.3)	65.5 (65.5 ± 1.5)
OpusMT-FT	29.6 (29.6 ± 1.4) (p = 0.0010)*	53.8 (53.8 ± 1.4) (p = 0.0010)*	**58.7 (58.7 ± 1.6) (p = 0.0010)***
NLLB-dist-600M	22.1 (22.1 ± 1.5) (p = 0.0480)*	48.4 (48.4 ± 1.3) (p = 0.2547)	68.9 (68.8 ± 4.2) (p = 0.0559)
NLLB-dist-600M-FT	**30.3 (30.3 ± 1.4) (p = 0.0010)***	**54.5 (54.5 ± 1.2) (p = 0.0010)***	**58.8 (58.8 ± 1.7) (p = 0.0010)***
GoogleT	27.1 (27.0 ± 1.1) (p = 0.0010)*	52.9 (52.9 ± 1.1) (p = 0.0010)*	61.0 (61.0 ± 1.4) (p = 0.0010)*
French-Croatian			
Baseline: OpusMT	14.2 (14.2 ± 1.0)	40.9 (40.9 ± 1.2)	74.6 (74.6 ± 1.3)
OpusMT-FT	**19.1 (19.1 ± 1.2) (p = 0.0010)***	**46.0 (46.1 ± 1.4) (p = 0.0010)***	**68.9 (68.9 ± 1.5) (p = 0.0010)***
NLLB-dist-600M	12.5 (12.5 ± 1.1) (p = 0.0010)*	40.5 (40.5 ± 1.0) (p = 0.1479)	79.8 (79.8 ± 3.1) (p = 0.0010)*
NLLB-dist-600M-FT	**18.8 (18.8 ± 1.1) (p = 0.0010)***	**46.3 (46.3 ± 1.2) (p = 0.0010)***	**69.4 (69.4 ± 1.4) (p = 0.0010)***
GoogleT	**18.7 (18.6 ± 1.2) (p = 0.0010)***	**47.0 (47.0 ± 1.1) (p = 0.0010)***	**69.8 (69.8 ± 1.3) (p = 0.0010)***
Croatian-French			
Baseline: OpusMT	20.3 (20.3 ± 1.1)	46.7 (46.7 ± 1.3)	71.4 (71.4 ± 1.5)
OpusMT-FT	**25.6 (25.6 ± 1.3) (p = 0.0010)***	**51.7 (51.7 ± 1.3) (p = 0.0010)***	**65.0 (65.0 ± 1.7) (p = 0.0010)***
NLLB-dist-600M	19.3 (19.2 ± 0.9) (p = 0.0120)*	47.2 (47.2 ± 0.8) (p = 0.1479)	74.1 (74.2 ± 1.3) (p = 0.0010)*
NLLB-dist-600M-FT	**26.0 (25.9 ± 1.3) (p = 0.0010)***	**51.7 (51.7 ± 1.2) (p = 0.0010)***	**65.6 (65.6 ± 1.7) (p = 0.0010)***
GoogleT	24.2 (24.2 ± 1.4) (p = 0.0010)*	**51.5 (51.4 ± 1.2) (p = 0.0010)***	67.7 (67.7 ± 1.6) (p = 0.0010)*
French-Catalan			
Baseline: OpusMT	24.1 (24.1 ± 1.2)	48.7 (48.7 ± 1.3)	64.7 (64.6 ± 1.6)
OpusMT-FT	34.0 (34.1 ± 1.6) (p = 0.0010)*	56.8 (56.9 ± 1.7) (p = 0.0010)*	54.4 (54.3 ± 2.1) (p = 0.0010)*
NLLB-dist-600M	25.3 (25.3 ± 2.0) (p = 0.0440)*	51.7 (51.7 ± 1.2) (p = 0.0010)*	66.8 (66.6 ± 6.2) (p = 0.1648)
NLLB-dist-600M-FT	**37.9 (37.9 ± 1.5) (p = 0.0010)***	**60.2 (60.3 ± 1.4) (p = 0.0010)***	**52.1 (52.0 ± 2.2) (p = 0.0010)***
GoogleT	33.3 (33.3 ± 1.6) (p = 0.0010)*	57.6 (57.6 ± 1.3) (p = 0.0010)*	55.0 (55.1 ± 1.6) (p = 0.0010)*
Catalan-French			
Baseline: OpusMT	24.3 (24.3 ± 1.1)	50.1 (50.2 ± 1.4)	66.1 (66.0 ± 1.7)
OpusMT-FT	33.3 (33.3 ± 1.5) (p = 0.0010)*	57.3 (57.4 ± 1.6) (p = 0.0010)*	56.7 (56.6 ± 2.1) (p = 0.0010)*
NLLB-dist-600M	28.1 (28.2 ± 1.4) (p = 0.0010)*	55.3 (55.3 ± 1.1) (p = 0.0010)*	64.7 (64.6 ± 4.2) (p = 0.1678)
NLLB-dist-600M-FT	**37.4 (37.4 ± 1.4) (p = 0.0010)***	**60.8 (60.9 ± 1.4) (p = 0.0010)***	**53.2 (53.1 ± 2.0) (p = 0.0010)***
GoogleT	33.4 (33.4 ± 2.1) (p = 0.0010)*	58.9 (58.9 ± 1.4) (p = 0.0010)*	56.4 (56.4 ± 2.1) (p = 0.0010)*

Table 2: Evaluation metrics for all language pairs

	Spanish-Croatian	**French-Catalan**
Base model	32	27
Fine-tuned model	**66**	**71**
Both	2	2
Total	100	100

Table 3: Results of the human evaluation

puts were judged to be of equal quality. These results align with the automatic evaluation metrics and support the conclusion that fine-tuning on the RomCro corpus improves MT output quality.

5 Conclusions and future work

This study has demonstrated the effectiveness of fine-tuning existing NMT models using RomCro v.2.0 for literary translation tasks. Our experiments confirm that the fine-tuned models consistently outperform baseline models and, in most cases, achieve results comparable to or better than Google Translate. These findings are supported by both automatic evaluation metrics and human assessments, reinforcing the value of domain-specific corpora for improving translation quality in literary contexts. The fine-tuning approach has shown particular promise for underrepresented language pairs, such as Spanish-Croatian, where the improvements in translation quality were substantial.

However, despite these advances, some challenges remain. While fine-tuning led to improved performance across all evaluated language pairs, certain discrepancies were noted, particularly in the translation of stylistically complex literary segments. This highlights the need for further refinements, including more targeted preprocessing and domain adaptation techniques. Additionally, the human evaluation process, though valuable, was limited in scope and should be expanded to include a larger number of segments, additional language pairs, and a more detailed qualitative analysis of translation errors.

For future work, we plan to expand human evaluation efforts by increasing the number of annotated segments and incorporating more translation directions. We will also conduct a more in-depth analysis of translation errors to identify specific linguistic phenomena where NMT models struggle. We also plan to use these fine-tuned models to produce bilingual e-books and pedagogical materials for language learners, leveraging the improved literary translations produced by the fine-tuned models.

6 Limitations of this study

One limitation of our study concerns the choice of evaluation metrics. While we primarily relied on automatic metrics such as BLEU, chrF2, and TER, we initially chose not to include COMET in our main evaluation pipeline. This decision was motivated by the fact that COMET's results depend heavily on the underlying model used and on the possibility of training custom models, both of which, in our view, warrant further investigation.

However, for the sake of completeness, we later computed COMET scores using the default model `wmt22-comet-da` to compare the systems evaluated in this study. The results, presented in the tables 4 to 9, confirm two main trends. First, Google Translate consistently achieves the highest COMET scores across all evaluated language pairs (except for the mean in the Catalan-French scenario, see table 9). Second, and importantly, our fine-tuned models show clear improvements over their respective baselines even under COMET evaluation, which reinforces the effectiveness of fine-tuning with RomCro v.2.0, regardless of the evaluation metric applied. These results provide further support for our conclusions and highlight the robustness of our approach.

We did not include the use of large language models (LLMs) for translation in our study for several reasons. First, the wide variety of available models and the strong dependency of translation quality on prompt design would require a detailed and systematic analysis, which we believe deserves a dedicated study and a separate publication. Second, fine-tuning large language models demands significantly more powerful computational resources than were available to us at the time of conducting this research.

Acknowledgments

This work was supported by the Croatian Science Foundation under the project number MOBODL-2023-08-9511, funded by the European Union – NextGenerationEU.

References

Gorana Bikić-Carić, Bojana Mikelenić, and Metka Bezlaj. 2023. Construcción del RomCro, un corpus paralelo multilingüe. *Procesamiento del lenguaje natural*, 70:99–110.

Ahmed El-Kishky, Vishrav Chaudhary, Francisco Guzmán, and Philipp Koehn. 2020. CCAligned: A Massive Collection of Cross-Lingual Web-Document Pairs. In *Proceedings of the 2020 Conference on Empirical Methods in Natural Language Processing (EMNLP)*, pages 5960–5969.

Ana Guerberof-Arenas and Antonio Toral. 2022. Creativity in translation. *Translation Spaces*, 11(2):184–212.

Damien Hansen and Emmanuelle Esperança-Rodier. 2022. Human-Adapted MT for Literary Texts: Reality or Fantasy? In *NeTTT 2022*, pages 178–190.

Marcin Junczys-Dowmunt, Roman Grundkiewicz, Tomasz Dwojak, Hieu Hoang, Kenneth Heafield, Tom Neckermann, Frank Seide, Ulrich Germann, Alham Fikri Aji, Nikolay Bogoychev, et al. 2018. Marian: Fast Neural Machine Translation in C++. In *Proceedings of ACL 2018, System Demonstrations*, pages 116–121.

Adam Kilgarriff, Vít Baisa, Jan Bušta, Miloš Jakubíček, Vojtěch Kovář, Jan Michelfeit, Pavel Rychlý, and Vít Suchomel. 2014. The Sketch Engine: ten years on. *Lexicography*, 1(1):7–36.

Philipp Koehn. 2020. *Neural machine translation*. Cambridge University Press.

Philipp Koehn, Hieu Hoang, Alexandra Birch, Chris Callison-Burch, Marcello Federico, Nicola Bertoldi, Brooke Cowan, Wade Shen, Christine Moran, Richard Zens, et al. 2007. Moses: Open source toolkit for statistical machine translation. In *Proceedings of the 45th annual meeting of the association for computational linguistics companion volume proceedings of the demo and poster sessions*, pages 177–180. Association for Computational Linguistics.

Marie-Aude Lefer. 2021. Parallel corpora. In *A practical handbook of corpus linguistics*, pages 257–282. Springer.

Els Lefever, Lieve Macken, and Veronique Hoste. 2009. Language-independent bilingual terminology extraction from a multilingual parallel corpus. In *Proceedings of the 12th Conference of the European Chapter of the ACL (EACL 2009)*, pages 496–504.

Clara Inés López Rodríguez. 2016. Using corpora in scientific and technical translation training: resources to identify conventionality and promote creativity. *Cadernos de traduçao*, 36:88–120.

Bojana Mikelenić and Antoni Oliver. 2024. Using a multilingual literary parallel corpus to train NMT systems. In *Proceedings of the 1st Workshop on Creative-text Translation and Technology*, pages 1–9.

Antoni Oliver. 2023. Author-tailored neural machine translation systems for literary works. In *Computer-Assisted Literary Translation*, pages 126–141. Routledge.

Kishore Papineni, Salim Roukos, Todd Ward, and Wei-Jing Zhu. 2002. Bleu: a method for automatic evaluation of machine translation. In *Proceedings of the 40th annual meeting of the Association for Computational Linguistics*, pages 311–318.

Maja Popović. 2015. chrF: character n-gram F-score for automatic MT evaluation. In *Proceedings of the tenth workshop on statistical machine translation*, pages 392–395.

Matt Post. 2018. A call for clarity in reporting BLEU scores. In *Proceedings of the Third Conference on Machine Translation: Research Papers*, pages 186–191, Belgium, Brussels. Association for Computational Linguistics.

Matthew Snover, Bonnie Dorr, Richard Schwartz, Linnea Micciulla, and John Makhoul. 2006. A study of translation edit rate with targeted human annotation. In *Proceedings of the 7th Conference of the Association for Machine Translation in the Americas: Technical Papers*, pages 223–231.

Antonio Toral, Andreas Van Cranenburgh, and Tia Nutters. 2023. Literary-Adapted Machine Translation in a Well-Resourced Language Pair: Explorations with More Data and Wider Contexts. In *Computer-Assisted Literary Translation*. Routledge. Num Pages: 26.

Antonio Toral and Andy Way. 2015. Machine-assisted translation of literary text: A case study. *Translation Spaces*, 4(2):240–267.

Appendices:

Metric signatures

- BLEU: nrefs:1 | bs:1000 | seed:12345 |case:mixed | eff:no | tok:13a | smooth:exp| version:2.4.3
- chrF2: nrefs:1 | bs:1000 | seed:12345 | case:mixed | eff:yes | nc:6 | nw:0 | space:no | version:2.4.3
- TER: nrefs:1 | bs:1000 | seed:12345 | case:lc | tok:tercom | norm:no | punct:yes | asian:no | version:2.4.3
- COMET: Unbabel/wmt22-comet-da

System	COMET Mean	vs. OpusMT	vs. OpusMT-FT	vs. NLLB200	vs. NLLB200-FT	vs. GoogleT
OpusMT	0.7863	-	F	T	F	F
OpusMT-FT	0.8180	T	-	T	T	F
NLLB200	0.7761	F	F	-	F	F
NLLB200-FT	0.8150	T	F	T	-	F
GoogleT	0.8343	T	T	T	T	-

Table 4: COMET mean scores and pairwise system comparisons for Spanish-Croatian. T indicates the system in the row outperforms the system in the column, F otherwise.

System	COMET Mean	vs. OpusMT	vs. OpusMT-FT	vs. NLLB200	vs. NLLB200-FT	vs. GoogleT
OpusMT	0.7697	-	F	F	F	F
OpusMT-FT	0.8011	T	-	T	F	F
NLLB200	0.7703	T	F	-	F	F
NLLB200-FT	0.8092	T	T	T	-	F
GoogleT	0.8124	T	T	T	T	-

Table 5: COMET mean scores and pairwise system comparisons for Croatian-Spanish. T indicates the system in the row outperforms the system in the column, F otherwise.

System	COMET Mean	vs. OpusMT	vs. OpusMT-FT	vs. NLLB200	vs. NLLB200-FT	vs. GoogleT
OpusMT	0.7738	-	F	T	F	F
OpusMT-FT	0.8060	T	-	T	F	F
NLLB200	0.7631	F	F	-	F	F
NLLB200-FT	0.8083	T	T	T	-	F
GoogleT	0.8238	T	T	T	T	-

Table 6: COMET mean scores and pairwise system comparisons for French-Croatian. T indicates the system in the row outperforms the system in the column, F otherwise.

System	COMET Mean	vs. OpusMT	vs. OpusMT-FT	vs. NLLB200	vs. NLLB200-FT	vs. GoogleT
OpusMT	0.7378	-	F	T	F	F
OpusMT-FT	0.7477	T	-	T	F	F
NLLB200	0.7319	F	F	-	F	F
NLLB200-FT	0.7725	T	T	T	-	F
GoogleT	0.7796	T	T	T	T	-

Table 7: COMET mean scores and pairwise system comparisons for Croatian-French. T indicates the system in the row outperforms the system in the column, F otherwise.

System	COMET Mean	vs. OpusMT	vs. OpusMT-FT	vs. NLLB200	vs. NLLB200-FT	vs. GoogleT
OpusMT	0.7104	-	F	F	F	F
OpusMT-FT	0.7698	T	-	T	F	F
NLLB200	0.7568	T	F	-	F	F
NLLB200-FT	0.7945	T	T	T	-	F
GoogleT	0.7973	T	T	T	T	-

Table 8: COMET mean scores and pairwise system comparisons for French-Catalan. T indicates the system in the row outperforms the system in the column, F otherwise.

System	COMET Mean	vs. OpusMT	vs. OpusMT-FT	vs. NLLB200	vs. NLLB200-FT	vs. GoogleT
OpusMT	0.6876	-	F	F	F	F
OpusMT-FT	0.7507	T	-	T	F	F
NLLB200	0.7377	T	F	-	F	F
NLLB200-FT	0.7950	T	T	T	-	F
GoogleT	0.7898	T	T	T	T	-

Table 9: COMET mean scores and pairwise system comparisons for Catalan-French. T indicates the system in the row outperforms the system in the column, F otherwise.

Can *Peter Pan* Survive MT? A Stylometric Study of LLMs, NMTs, and HTs in Children's Literature Translation

Delu Kong[1,2] and Lieve Macken[2]

[1]School of Foreign Studies, Tongji University, Shanghai, 200092, China
[2]Language and Translation Technology Team, Ghent University, Ghent, 9000, Belgium
Correspondence: kongdelu2009@hotmail.com

Abstract

This study focuses on evaluating the performance of machine translations (MTs) compared to human translations (HTs) in English-to-Chinese children's literature translation (CLT) from a stylometric perspective. The research constructs a Peter Pan corpus, comprising 21 translations: 7 human translations (HTs), 7 large language model translations (LLMs), and 7 neural machine translation outputs (NMTs). The analysis employs a generic feature set (including lexical, syntactic, readability, and n-gram features) and a creative text translation (CTT-specific) feature set, which captures repetition, rhythm, translatability, and miscellaneous levels, yielding 447 linguistic features in total.

Using classification and clustering techniques in machine learning, we conduct a stylometric analysis of these translations. Results reveal that in generic features, HTs and MTs exhibit significant differences in conjunction word distributions and the ratio of 1-word-gram-一样, while NMTs and LLMs show significant variation in descriptive words usage and adverb ratios. Regarding CTT-specific features, LLMs outperform NMTs in distribution, aligning more closely with HTs in stylistic characteristics, demonstrating the potential of LLMs in CLT.

1 Introduction

With the advent of LLMs[1] , various evaluations have been made within user and researcher communities (Jiao et al., 2023; Castilho et al., 2023; Enis and Hopkins, 2024). A consensus has been reached: LLMs appear to be useful for handling texts that use highly formulaic language, such as contracts, technical documents, and web pages. However, when it comes to translating highly creative texts, such as literary works, it remains a highly challenging task (Kocmi et al., 2024).

Among all text types, literary texts serve as a formidable "bastion" (Toral and Way, 2014) that challenge the performance of MT engines. Compared to informational texts, literary texts place greater emphasis on aesthetic creation. They are characterized by intricate linguistic structures, rich metaphors, and deep cultural nuances, interwoven with the styles of different nations, cultures, eras, and even individual authors (Hadley et al., 2022). Therefore, literary translation not only facilitates the cross-linguistic transmission of ideas but also needs to recreate the artistic charm of the original work. As some scholars have pointed out, the innovative nature of literary texts "almost implies an inherent degree of resistance to automation" (Ruffo, 2022, p. 18), which also creates tricky challenges for MT developers seeking effective solutions.

As a significant branch of literary translation, children's literature translation (CLT for abbreviation) inspires limitless imagination in young readers worldwide. The choice to research CLT arises from its distinctive combination of literary artistry and creative expression: (1) it is crucial for cultural exchange and dissemination of children literature worldwide; (2) children's literature often features relatively unique expressions, making it ideal for assessing MT systems' semantic and cultural handling; (3) evaluating MT performance is vital to prevent mistranslations or hallucinations that could mislead young readers early on.

2 Related work

2.1 Stylometric investigation in CLT studies

Over the past decade, the field of CLT studies has expanded significantly. Scholars note that the

[1]MT is used as a superordinate term encompassing both NMT and LLM translation, while NMT and LLM can also be treated as distinct categories based on the underlying generation engines.

Proceedings of the Second Workshop on Creative-text Translation and Technology (CTT), pages 52–70, June 24, 2025

first two decades of the 21st century have been a "blooming period" for research on translating children's books (Fornalczyk-Lipska, 2022). Once a marginal topic, it is now recognized that CLT works become a crucial part in young readers' literary experiences worldwide (Van Coillie and McMartin, 2020). Puurtinen (2003) was among the pioneering scholars who employed a corpus-based methodology to investigate CLT. Her study examines translation-specific features in Finnish children's literature, identifying a high frequency of non-finite structures, a relative absence of colloquial expressions as potential hallmarks of translated texts.

In recent years, the study of CLT has witnessed more refined outputs within the framework of stylometry or quantitative stylistics[2]. Čermáková (2018) uses corpus-based method to analyse the feature of repetition in CLT, showing that translators often find repetition uncomfortable and tend to compensate for it by using synonymy. For the Chinese-English language pair, Zhang et al. (2019) examine increased lexical-grammatical explicitness in Chinese CLT, and show a higher frequency of personal pronouns compared to non-translated texts, likely due to cross-linguistic influence from the source language. Also, Zhao et al. (2022) explore how narrative space is transferred in CLT from Chinese works to English translated versions, and show that selective appropriation (patterns of omission and addition designed to suppress, accentuate or elaborate particular aspects of a narrative) is the most used strategy.

The aforementioned studies have established a foundation for applying stylometric analysis to CLT. However, compared to general translation studies, where broad features such as Type-token-ratio (TTR), PoS-tags, and word frequencies are commonly analyzed (see Päpcke et al., 2022; Ding, 2024; Ploeger et al., 2024), CTT-features are more specifically utilized in CLT studies and are less frequently examined in broader translation research. CLT requires attention to more specific aspects, including repetition, metaphor, and rhythmic patterns. To address this, the present study incorporates both generic stylometric features and those specifically tailored to CLT, which are presented in Section 3.2.

[2]In this paper, stylometry is used interchangeably with quantitative stylistics, both referring to approaches that emphasize feature engineering and statistical analysis of textual style. In contrast, stylistics more broadly involves interpretive analysis of how language produces meaning, literary effects, and context-sensitive nuances.

2.2 MT in creative texts

MT's application in creative texts raises debates on its impact on the accuracy of cultural and creative expression. Even before the advent of NMT, Toral and Way (2014) raised the question of the usefulness of MT for literature. The very next year, Toral and Way (2015) demonstrated that a statistical machine translation system adapted to literary texts outperformed generic baseline systems, and could be further incorporated into the literary translator's workflow.

The NMT system advancement has sparked growing interest among scholars in applying MT to literary texts. Toral and Way (2018) evaluate NMT for literary texts, specifically novels, and find that NMT achieves an 11% relative improvement in BLEU scores compared with statistical MT. Yet if we look at literary translators' attitudes, the story is different. Studies show more experienced literary translators prefer translating from scratch, and might be resistant in using NMTs for more freedom (Moorkens et al., 2018; Way et al., 2023). From a reader perspective, Guerberof-Arenas and Toral (2024) observed that, in a case study of different translations, the MT version, compared to HT and PE, received the lowest ratings for narrative understanding and attentional focus, with structural and lexical issues contributing to a disrupted and confusing reading experience.

This raises the question: why are MT outputs often not well received by translators and readers? One major issue lies in stylistic limitations. Daems (2022) points out that MT systems struggle with capturing stylistic nuances, humour, and contextual or cultural subtleties—elements widely recognized as central to the nature of literary texts. Farrell (2018) and Taivalkoski-Shilov (2018) both emphasize that MT or post-edited output may result in homogenization and normalization in the target texts, trends that run counter to the diverse and creative nature of literary texts. Several studies investigate the stylistic difference between HTs and NMTs of literary works. For example, Jiang and Niu (2022) show that NMTs might be less coherent in discourse and less consistent in lexical choices. A more recent study also shows that NMT outputs can be distinguished from the HT counterparts based on sentence length distribution (Rybicki, 2025). These studies inspired us to follow a similar vein and examine whether LLM outputs differ from those of NMT systems.

2.3 Research gaps and questions

Summarizing the above studies, despite the solid foundation of CLT research, stylometric methods remain underexplored. Additionally, while existing studies of MT on literary works predominantly focus on general literary works, children's literature has received comparatively less attention. This gap underscores the need for research that accounts for the unique linguistic characteristics of CLT. Furthermore, the translation capabilities of LLM systems have gained significant interest; however, most research in this domain remains centered on NMT engines. The effectiveness of LLMs in CLT needs further investigation.

Based on these gaps, our study focuses on CLT among three translation groups, namely HTs, NMTs and LLMs. We construct a large dataset by incorporating a total of 21 English to Chinese translations of *Peter Pan*, and establish a more comprehensive feature set with a sub-category tailored for CTT. We adopt the research design of Daems et al. (2017) and Lynch and Vogel (2018), and collect experimental results and draw salient features, and then compare inter- and intra-group performance.

We address the following research questions:

- RQ1: Do MTs differ from HTs in CLT on generic textual features and CTT-specific features?
- RQ2: Do LLM outputs differ from NMT outputs in CLT on generic textual features and CTT-specific features?
- RQ3: How do salient features illustrate the differences among HTs, NMTs, and LLMs in CLT?

3 Methodology

3.1 Dataset

The corpus used in this study is based on J.M. Barrie's 1911 novel *Peter and Wendy*, the classic children's version of the Peter Pan story[3]. The character of Peter Pan was first introduced in Barrie's 1902 novel *The Little White Bird*. The 1911 novel has been widely cherished by children worldwide for its vivid imagination and the thrilling adventures of Peter Pan. The HTs are selected from **7** Chinese translations published by reputable publishers, spanning a wide time range (1929–2020) to ensure representativeness across different eras.

For MTs, the translated texts are categorized into two groups: NMTs and LLMs, with **7** engines selected for each category to produce a total of **14** MTed versions. In the NMT category, while some providers have reportedly begun integrating LLM technologies into their traditional NMT systems, e.g. DeepL[4], this study specifically aims to examine "pure" NMTs. To achieve this goal, models that explicitly state using an NMT engine are prioritized. For providers offering multiple MT engine versions, the NMT variant is selected whenever possible. If no version details were disclosed, the default engine is used. All NMTs are accessed via API. Details can be viewed in the online supplementary materials.

For LLMs, we select state-of-the-art commercial generic models, such as ChatGPT and Claude, as well as open-sourced DeepSeek, and MT-tailored LaraTranslate, and both open-sourced and MT-tailored Unbabel-TowerInstruct. Large-parameter deep reasoning models such as GPT-o1 and DeepSeek-R1, though strong in contextless multilingual translation, are not adopted in our framework due to their high inference cost, slower processing speed, and tendency to generate rambling outputs in Chinese (Chen et al., 2025). These factors significantly increase computational complexity and reduce overall efficiency in translation tasks. Consequently, we prioritize LLM models optimized for faster, more direct translation processes.

The MT process for LLMs involves prompt engineering, adhering to practices outlined in Andrew Ng's course[5] and the CRISPE framework[6]. This ensures a structured and standardized prompt design, consistently applied across all engines during translation. The complete prompt used in our experiments is provided in Appendix A for reference. Furthermore, we distinguish between MT engines developed by Chinese and non-Chinese enterprises, as this distinction may influence translation strategies and quality, particularly given that Chinese is the target language.

All texts underwent rigorous preprocessing, in-

[3]The 1911 novel uniquely includes the final chapter "When Wendy Grew Up", which does not appear in play or later abridged versions. This chapter is present in all Chinese translations used in this study. Although some translations do not explicitly state the source text, the inclusion of this chapter indicates that all were ultimately based on the 1911 novel.

[4]https://www.smartling.com/blog/how-accurate-is-deepl

[5]https://learn.deeplearning.ai/courses/chatgpt-prompt-eng

[6]https://github.com/mattnigh/ChatGPT3-Free-Prompt-List

Type	Translator	Abbr.	Engine	Acquisition	Token	Type	Sent.	Year
Source	-	-	-	E-book	47,978	5,334	3,334	2005
HTs	Liang	HTL	-	OCR	47,627	5,108	3,229	1929
	Yang & Gu	HYG	-	E-book	50,222	5,798	3,500	1991
	Ren	HTR	-	E-book	51,271	4,968	3,424	2006
	Ma	HTM	-	E-book	47,777	5,358	3,662	2011
	Sun	HSU	-	E-book	56,674	5,872	3,673	2017
	Shi	HSH	-	E-book	50,451	5,220	3,571	2018
	Huang	HTH	-	E-book	51,233	5,477	3,937	2020
NMTs	DeepL	NDL	Classic	API	46,731	4,980	2,850	2025 Feb.
	GoogleTrans	NGT	v2	API	46,891	4,887	3,268	
	MicrosoftTrans	NMS	-	API	46,854	4,711	3,150	
	AmazonTrans	NAZ	-	API	46,097	4,599	3,206	
	BaiduTrans*	NBD	-	API	45,697	4,514	3,205	
	YoudaoTrans*	NYD	-	API	47,817	4,690	3,393	
	NiuTrans*	NNT	-	API	46,296	4,541	3,197	
LLMs	ChatGPT	LCG	4o	Web	50,958	5,965	3,980	2025 Feb.
	Claude	LCL	3.5-sonnet	Web	46,503	5,355	3,426	
	Gemini	LGM	1.5-flash	API	48,174	5,489	3,474	
	Kimi*	LKM	v1	API	57,320	5,221	3,869	
	DeepSeek*	LDS	v3	OpenSource	45,951	4,865	3,421	
	TowerInstruct	LTI	7b-v0.2	OpenSource	46,097	4,869	3,124	
	LaraTrans	LLT	Creative	Web	48,576	4,709	3,176	
Total	-	-	-	-	**1,025,217**	**107,196**	**71,735**	-

Table 1: Overview of the datasets used in this study. Pure NMT version is selected if the provider offers version options (such as NDL and NGT). LaraTranslate provides a "creative text" style option but, despite claiming to use LLM technology, does not support custom prompts. Engines marked with * are developed by Chinese enterprises. The total count excludes the source text.

cluding cleaning, denoising, part-of-speech (PoS) tagging, and dependency (Dep) parsing. Since Chinese lacks explicit word boundaries, prior word segmentation is necessary. To achieve SOTA performance, we utilize the Language Technology Platform (LTP)[7], a comprehensive natural language processing toolkit (Che et al., 2021). LTP's deep learning model (Base2) is used for word segmentation, PoS tagging, and syntactic analysis, achieving reported accuracies of 99.18%, 98.69%, and 90.19% for these tasks, respectively.[8]

The final *Peter Pan* translation corpus exceeds over one million tokens. A detailed overview of the dataset is provided in Table 1.

3.2 Feature set

Based on the principles to construct feature set for stylometric analysis (Volansky et al., 2013)[9] and referring to previous research (see Huang and Liu, 2009; Lynch and Vogel, 2018; Toral, 2019; De Clercq et al., 2021), the following section presents the feature set applied in this study. A brief feature summary is in Table 3 (in Appendix B). All together, we've employed 447 features in this study. It should be noted that all features are represented as ratios or weighted measures to mitigate the influence of sample size differences and ensure comparability across texts.

3.2.1 Generic textual features

The generic textual features are designed to capture text characteristics from a holistic perspective. "Generic" means that these features are commonly used in other types of stylometric studies, not constrained on CLT studies. They are divided into four linguistic dimensions: lexical, syntactical, readability, and N-gram features.

Lexical features reflect word-level characteristics on lexical diversity, density, and richness, such as TTR. Additionally, PoS tag features, extracted using the LTP platform[10], capture the distribution of word classes, such as nouns and verbs.

Syntactic features focus on overall sentence structure and syntactic patterns, including average sentence length. Dependency tags are used

[7] `https://github.com/HIT-SCIR/ltp`

[8] `https://github.com/HIT-SCIR/ltp/blob/main/README.md`

[9] Although the quoted research focuses on translationese study, their proposed principles are highly relevant to construct a well-balanced and interpretable feature set for studying linguistic features of translated texts.

[10] `https://ltp.ai/docs/appendix.html#id2`

to further analyze syntactic roles, such as Mean Dependency Distance and the ratio of head and node.

Readability features include nine readability metrics proposed by Lei et al. (2024)[11], which evaluate lexical, syntactic, and semantic variability to assess a text's difficulty and comprehensibility for the target audience. Moreover, four concreteness features are included, measuring lexical concreteness based on the work of Xu and Li (2020).

N-gram features utilize N-word-grams and N-PoS-grams, where N ranges from 1 to 3, to capture locally constrained phrasal patterns. These features are extracted by comparing the target corpus with the LCMC reference corpus[12]. To maintain consistency, LCMC was re-tagged using the same LTP tools to ensure a uniform PoS-tag set.

3.2.2 CTT-specific features

CTT-specific features refer to characteristics specifically designed for creative text translation. In this study, we incorporate insights from previous Chinese research on CLT. These features are tailored to the linguistic and stylistic elements of CLT and are categorized into four subcategories:

Repetition features are a widely recognized in CLT, as a narrative strategy, often used to capture young readers' attention (Mastropierro, 2022). In this study, repetition features include AA-pattern (two-character repetition), AAA-pattern (three-character repetition), and ABAB-pattern structures.

Rhythm features examine phonetic patterns within the text, as previous research has identified distinct rhythmic patterns in CLT (Cooper, 1989). This study captures key rhythm features, such as rhyme proportion, vowel balance, and tonal alternation.

Translatibility features[13] assess language transfer and translation completeness between the source and the target texts through five key aspects: completeness, foreignness, code-switching, abbreviation, and untranslatable elements. Notably, completeness identifies untranslated English phrases longer than three words, while foreignness measures the ratio of English to Chinese characters.

The miscellaneous category includes five unique linguistic features that could not satisfactorily fall into the previous classifications but are frequently observed in CLT. These include the proportion of onomatopoeia, the usage of the Chinese-specific "-er suffix"[14], and the frequency of sentence-final particles, among others.

We put more detailed explanations and examples in the supplementary materials.

3.3 Algorithms

3.3.1 Feature selection

To streamline the experiment, mitigate feature noise, and enhance efficiency, we adopt a feature selection strategy based on chi-square (χ^2) ranking in both classification and clustering tasks. Features are prioritized according to their χ^2 values, with the top 30 being retained. If a given category contains fewer than 30 features, all available ones are preserved.

3.3.2 Classification experiment

The classification experiment follows a hierarchical structure based on different feature set levels. Initially, classification is performed separately for each feature sub-level. The experimental setup consists of the following comparison groups: (1) HTs vs. MTs, where MTs encompass both NMTs and LLMs; (2) HTs vs. NMTs and LLMs separately; (3) LLMs vs. NMTs; and (4) intra-group classification within the NMTs and LLMs categories.

To evaluate classification performance, five classifiers are employed: Naïve Bayes, Logistic Regression, Support Vector Machine (SVM), Decision Tree, and Random Forest. The average performance across these classifiers is reported. The SVM model is configured with a linear kernel, while the remaining classifiers use their default settings. Following the methodology outlined by Rahman et al. (2024), the effectiveness of the ensemble classifier is assessed using Accuracy (ACC) score. All classification tasks, except intra-group classifications within the NMTs and LLMs groups, are binary classification tasks.

[11] https://github.com/leileibama/AlphaReadabilityChinese

[12] https://www.lancaster.ac.uk/fass/projects/corpus/LCMC/

[13] We categorize translatability features under the CTT-specific level, considering that CLT is particularly sensitive to language shifts. This sensitivity is especially pronounced when the target audience is mainly children. The interweaving of English elements within Chinese text might influence their reading experience.

[14] The "-er suffix" in Chinese is a linguistic phenomenon where the suffix "儿" (ér) is added to the end of a word, often altering its pronunciation and adding a diminutive meaning. This is widely used in spoken and literary Chinese. For example, 花 (huā, "flower") becomes 花儿 (huār), and 鸟 (niǎo, "bird") becomes 鸟儿 (niǎor).

3.3.3 Clustering experiment

The clustering experiment employs the k-means algorithm to categorize data. Rather than predefining the number of clusters (k), it is determined based on performance evaluation. Euclidean distance serves as the similarity metric for clustering, and the feature set is derived from the Top-k features identified in the earlier analysis.

To assess clustering effectiveness, the Adjusted Rand Index (ARI) is used as the primary evaluation metric. ARI quantifies the alignment between the clustering results and ground truth labels while accounting for chance, providing an objective measure of clustering quality (Warrens and van der Hoef, 2022). Beyond numerical evaluation, interactive clustering visualizations are generated using Python's Plotly library.

In addition to k-means clustering, hierarchical clustering is introduced as a complementary approach. This method utilizes the stylo package in R, incorporating the top 100 most frequent words and Eder's delta (Eder, 2015) as key metrics. By integrating multiple clustering strategies, we aim to strengthen the robustness of our analysis and enhance the overall reliability of the experimental findings.

4 Results

4.1 Classification

Level	Sub-level	HTs -MTs	HTs -NMTs	HTs -LLMs	NMTs -LLMs
Generic textual features	Lexical	0.8673	0.9149	0.8526	0.7439
	Syntactical	0.8001	0.8443	0.7128	0.6752
	Readability	0.6645	0.7056	0.5538	0.6178
	N-gram	0.8674	0.8803	0.8486	0.7724
CTT-specific features	Repetition	0.6274	0.6800	0.5778	0.5436
	Rhythm	0.6650	0.5564	0.6444	0.5593
	Translatibility	0.6883	0.7930	0.6091	0.6067
	Miscellaneous	0.7378	0.7521	0.6393	0.6172
All	-	0.9149	0.9376	0.8896	0.7464

Table 2: Classification results across different feature levels and comparison groups. "Generic textual features" encompass general linguistic attributes, while "CTT-specific features" focus on aspects relevant to creative text translation. "All" represents the combined performance when all features are used together.

Table 2 presents the results across feature levels and groups. It should be noted that a high ACC score indicates a clear distinction between the examined categories, while a low ACC score suggests greater similarity. We generalize two tendencies:

First, from group comparison perspective, HTs consistently achieve the highest performance across different pairwise comparisons, with HTs-NMTs reaching the highest accuracy (0.9376) and HTs-MTs following closely (0.9149). When LLMs are involved, accuracy drops, as seen in HTs-LLMs (0.8896) and NMTs-LLMs (0.7464). This suggests that distinguishing between HTs and other MTed translations (NMTs and LLMs) is relatively easier, while differentiating within the same category (intra-group) is much harder, as in HTs (0.6785), NMTs (0.5965), and LLMs (0.5917).

Second, from feature categories perspective, among the generic textual features, lexical and N-gram features contribute the most to classification, with the highest ACC across different translation types (e.g., HTs-NMTs: 0.9149 and 0.8803, respectively). Readability exhibits the lowest performance, as in HTs-LLMs (0.5538). Regarding CTT-specific features, translatability and miscellaneous features contribute notably in differentiating HTs from other groups, while repetition and rhythm drop sharply in ACC scores. Overall, generic features perform better than CTT-specific features in classification, and using all features leads to the best performance.

Figure 1 (in Appendix D) presents a pairwise classification heatmap to provide a visualized plot and a fine-grained classifying result. It reveals three main results:

First, for HTs, the classification accuracy between HTs and other groups (NMTs and LLMs) is generally high. Within the HTs group, the highest ACC exceeds 0.90. The highest intra-group accuracy is observed in the HTL-HTH pair (0.98), also HTL achieves the highest average ACC (0.97) compared with all other samples. This may be due to the significant temporal gap, as HTL is the earliest translation among HTs. Conversely, the HSU-HTM and HSU-HTR pairs (both 0.76) exhibit the lowest accuracy, with HSU having the lowest average ACC (0.87). The greater similarities among these translations might be newer versions drawing references from previously published ones.

Second, for NMTs, ACC in distinguishing NMTs-LLMs is relatively lower than that of NMTs-HTs, meaning NMTs are much more similar to LLMs in style. The lowest inter-group ACC is observed in NGT-LDS (0.59). The score within the NMTs group is considerably lower than that within the HTs group. The highest intra-group accuracy is

NAZ-NYD (0.94), while the lowest is NBD-NGT (0.44). Also, in terms of average ACC, we found that NAZ (0.92) and NDL (0.9) achieve relatively higher compared with the rest NMT engines, while NGT (0.79) is the lowest.

Third, within the LLM group, the highest intra-group ACC is observed in LCG-LLT (0.99), and LKM-LLT (0.65) exhibits the lowest. Still, on average ACC, LCG (0.96) and LCL (0.93) have the relative highest score compared with other LLM engines, while LDS (0.83) has the lowest one. No significant differences are found between MT systems developed by Chinese companies and those by international companies.

4.2 Clustering

Figure 2 presents the clustering results using K-means (left) and hierarchical clustering (right). The K-means clustering, with an ARI score of 0.4873, demonstrates a clear separation between HTs and NMTs, as the two groups are positioned far apart. However, LLMs exhibit a more complex distribution, which cannot be clustered into a distinct group. Notably, three LLMs (LCG, LCL, LGM) cluster closer to HTs, suggesting that their translations share more similarities with human translations. Meanwhile, a subset of LLMs (LKM, LDS, LLT, LTI) aligns more closely with NMTs.

The hierarchical clustering (right) supports these findings, displaying relatively stable and well-separated clusters for HTs and NMTs. In contrast, LLMs show a more dispersed pattern, with samples integrating into both HT and NMT clusters. This reveals that LLMs exhibit heterogeneous translation characteristics, with some models leaning towards human-like translation styles and others resembling NMT outputs. Both clustering results reinforce observations drawn from previous classification experiments.

5 Discussion

5.1 Overview from generic features

This section discusses these differences from the perspective of generic features and provides an overview on their variance.

5.1.1 Ratio of conjunctions

From Table 4, we can see that conjunction words and N-grams contribute greatly to the separation of HTs and MTs. For the ratio of conjunction words (Figure 3), HTs differ significantly from MTs, with MTs exhibiting a higher ratio (ANOVA F = 91.10, $p < 0.0001$)[15]. Among conjunction words, the 1-word-gram-然后 (English: then) serves as a good example, since it is particularly prominent, and exhibits a similar trend on its over-usage in MT outputs. It means that MTs tend to rely more on explicit logical connectors, exhibiting a certain tendency toward "explicitation" (Zhang et al., 2019), whereas HTs demonstrate greater flexibility in expression and are not strictly bound by the logical transitions of the source text. However, no significant difference is observed between NMTs and LLMs in terms of conjunction (p = 0.06).

5.1.2 Ratio of 1-word-gram-一样

Another feature that distinguishes HTs and MTs apart is the 1-word-gram-一样 (same). This word frequently follows another word to form a Chinese phrase "像...一样 (same as...)" which conveys a simile meaning. As shown in Figure 4, MTs exhibit a significantly higher frequency of "一样" compared to HTs (p < 0.0001), indicating that MTs tend to produce more explicit comparative structures. Particularly NMTs use "像...一样" more frequently. Hence, MTs are more constrained by source text structures and produce similar patterns, leading to potential 'homogenisation' (Daems et al., 2024) in lexical terms with less variation in figurative expressions. But for LLMs, we see that LCG (ChatGPT) and LCL (Claude) use relatively less "像...一样". Given that the principle of fidelity to source texts should be generally maintained in translation, the reduction in "像...一样" likely reflects a shift in how figurative meaning is expressed in the LLM translations, rather than a loss of figurative content.

Drawing on actual concordance as an example (see Figure 8), we observe that in HTs, there are only two occurrences of "像...一样", while other variations, such as "像...似的" and "宛如", are also used creatively. In contrast, all seven NMT outputs employ the same fixed expression, whereas LLMs exhibit a mix, with three outputs using the same phrase.

5.1.3 Ratio of descriptive and adverbial words

Figure 5 illustrates two important features that show significant differences between NMTs and LLMs. For the proportion of descriptive words (ratio_dscrptW), texts translated by LLMs exhibit

[15]To determine significant differences, we first conduct a normality test on the data. If the data met the normality assumption, we apply ANOVA; otherwise, we use the non-parametric Kruskal-Wallis test.

a significantly higher usage of descriptive expressions than NMTs ($p < 0.0001$). Since descriptive words are generally regarded as enhancing textual vividness and specificity by providing richer contextual details, their higher occurrence in LLMs suggests more expressive and stylistically nuanced outputs than NMTs. Second, the proportion of adverbs (ratio_adverb) across HTs, NMT, and LLM indicates significant differences among these three systems ($p < 0.0001$). The trend suggests that HTs employ adverbs more frequently than MTs, where LLM restores some adverb usage compared to NMT.

5.2 Zooming into CTT-specifc features

If we narrow down our analysis to a more specific CLT perspective, we can see from Table 4 that several CTT-specific features also stand out in distinguishing different translation groups.

5.2.1 Ratio of foreignness

To begin with, the left column of Figure 6 presents the foreignness feature at the level of translatability. By definition, this feature quantifies the ratio of English words that appeared in the translated text. HTs exhibit zero occurrence of the retained foreign words. In contrast, MTs, particularly NMTs, demonstrate a notably higher ratio. Interestingly, LLMs display a substantially lower foreignness ratio compared to NMT, approaching HT-like tendencies.

Most untranslated cases are names (Such as "其次是Slightly" in NBD; "Tink确实又开始四处乱窜" in NGT), and idiomatic expressions ("他与他们分道扬way了" in NAZ). Although this is less common in LLMs, some expressions are still translated incompletely ("他们 perfectly safe，不是吗？" in LGM), a type of error also pointed out by Macken (2024). For child readers, minimizing source-language element leakage in CLT is a way both to improve acceptability and to mitigate "cultural colonialism" , since children's limited experience may necessitate a higher degree of adaptation than adult fiction (Lathey, 2015, p. 38). In this regard, LLMs demonstrate an advantage over NMTs.

5.2.2 Ratio of er-suffix

For the "ratio_er_suffix" feature, as shown in the middle column of Figure 6, the upper graph indicates that HTs employ significantly more "-er suffixes" than MTs, while in the lower graph, LLMs exhibit a higher ratio compared to NMTs.

The "-er suffix" serves as an important figurative expression in CLT, as it often conveys a colloquial, playful, or affectionate tone. It is commonly used in northern Chinese dialects, particularly in Beijing (see Chen, 2000; Fu, 2022). Such phonetic modifications cater to children's cognitive development and linguistic preferences, making texts more engaging and accessible. Based on this, HTs remain the most effective in preserving "-er suffix" in CLT. However, prompt-tuned LLMs demonstrate a stronger ability to capture "-er suffix" features compared to NMTs, suggesting that LLMs are more aligned with HTs in this aspect.

5.2.3 Ratio of repetitive expression

Repetitive expressions, such as AA (e.g., "热热的" warm and cozy), AAA (e.g., "慢慢慢" very slowly), and ABAB (e.g., "很久很久" a very long period), are a prominent stylistic feature in children's literature. The ratio_AA[16] feature in the right column of Figure 6 indicates that HTs employ significantly more repetition than MTs, while LLMs outperform NMTs in preserving this pattern. Research has shown that repetitive structures enhance readability, reinforce linguistic patterns, and facilitate memory retention for young readers, making texts more engaging and accessible (Tannen, 1989; Hickmann, 2003). Given these, the results suggest that LLMs better capture the stylistic and cognitive functions of repetition in CLT than NMTs, making them more aligned with HTs.

5.3 Some further remarks on the LLM translations

5.3.1 On LCG and LCL

Figure 1 shows that two LLM-based engines, LCG (ChatGPT) and LCL (Claude) exhibit significant distinctions in pair-wise classification compared to HTs and other MTs. By examining the feature importance list in the classification logs, we observe that LCG demonstrates exceptionally high divergence in the *Average Number of Children per Node* feature (see Figure 7), exceeding the values of other texts by approximately 1.5 times. Specifically, HT averages around 20, while LCG reaches approximately 35.

This feature reflects the syntactic dependency tree structure, where a higher value suggests LCG favors a flatter syntactic structure rather than a deeply nested one. LCG appears to prioritize paral-

[16]It should be noted that the AA pattern mentioned here excludes fixed proper nouns, such as "妈妈 mom".

lelism and broader phrase expansion. Corpus analysis (see online supplementary material) further corroborates this pattern where LCG tends to segment sentences more frequently, breaking complex structures into multiple shorter clauses deliberately, perhaps in order to retain readability suitable to children's levels.

Subsequently, we observed that LCL exhibits a significantly higher deviation in the ratio_quote (quotation mark) feature, reaching approximately twice the value of other engines (see Figure 7). While other LLMs maintain an average ratio of 0.13, LCL reaches approximately 0.25. Although *Peter Pan* is a children's novel rich in dialogue, such an unusually high occurrence of quotation marks appears atypical.

Upon inspecting the corpus, we found that other LLMs use directional Chinese quotation marks, whereas LCL employs non-directional English quotation marks. Our quotation-matching process was designed to recognize left quotation mark and non-directional mark, but not for right quotation mark. This explains why LCL's quotation mark count is nearly double that of other models. However, in formal writing, Chinese translations should adhere to standard typographic conventions, using directional Chinese quotation marks. In this regard, LCL's handling of punctuation is less consistent with formal Chinese writing norms compared to other engines.

5.3.2 On LDS, LTI and LLT

In this section, we discuss in more detail the recent open-source engine LDS (DeepSeek) and MT-tailored engine LLT (LaraTranslate), and both MT-tailored and open-sourced engine LTI (Unbabel Tower_instruct).

The three engines exhibit a high degree of confusion with other MT engines in classification tasks, with LDS and NGT achieving classification accuracies of only 0.59 and 0.66 with NBD, respectively. While these engines (particularly LDS) have gained significant attention recently, a more critical evaluation reveals that their performance in MT tasks shows no substantial improvement compared to other LLM-based engines.

Among MT-tailored LLMs, LLT and LTI fail to reach a satisfactory level in CTT-specific features with notably poorer performance than other commercial LLM models (see Figure 7). Specifically, they exhibit lower usage of the "-er suffix" and fewer repetitive expressions. Despite LLT's popularity and its advertised "creative translation" capabilities, our analysis finds little evidence of enhanced stylistic performance in its output. Additionally, during our testing, LLT produced a significant number of hallucinations, and its trans_foreignness score was the highest.

Some marketing claims about certain LLMs should be critically evaluated rather than taken at face value. While some models may perform well in general machine translation tasks, their effectiveness in specialized domains—such as children's literature—requires thorough empirical validation.

6 Conclusion

This study investigates the extent to which MTs diverge from HTs in CLT from a stylometric perspective, focusing on both generic textual features and CTT-specific features.

For RQ1, our findings confirm that MTs exhibit significant differences from HTs across both feature sets. Looking at generic text features, MTs deviate from HTs in conjunction word distributions and the ratio of 1-word-grams, where MTs tend to favor literal translation strategies, with a stronger influence from the source text. Looking at CTT-specific features, MTs generally fail to reproduce stylistic elements crucial in CLT, such as repetition and "-er suffix", further reiterating the challenges of automated translation in preserving literary expressiveness.

For RQ2, NMTs and LLMs diverge notably in both generic and CTT-specific stylistic features. While LLMs and NMTs exhibit significant differences in descriptive word usage and adverb ratios, LLMs show greater alignment with HTs. LLMs also outperform NMTs in "-er suffix" usage, AA-pattern repetition, and foreignness. Thus, they are better and more effective at capturing stylistic patterns in CLT than NMTs.

For RQ3, our analysis reveals distinct stylistic differences among HTs, NMTs, and LLMs. HTs still act as the gold standard in stylistic expressions, while NMTs produce more rigid and less engaging outputs. LLMs strike a balance, with greater stylistic fluidity than NMTs and approximating HT-like translation patterns. However, performance varies across LLMs. ChatGPT and Claude exhibit stronger stylistic consistency, whereas open-sourced or MT-tailored models show no clear advantages over the rest.

Limitations and future work

This study has several limitations that future research should address:

First, in terms of dataset selection, this study is limited to a single literary work, *Peter Pan*, which, while representative, may not fully capture the diversity of children's literature. Future research should expand the dataset to include translations of varied genres and styles to improve generalizability. Moreover, it should be noted that the training data of LLMs may contain human translations of *Peter Pan*, potentially influencing the results and blurring the boundaries between human and LLM translations.

Second, methodologically, this study primarily relies on quantitative stylometric analysis, offering a broad "distant reading" of translation patterns. However, it lacks in-depth qualitative analysis to explain why certain stylistic deviations occur between HTs, LLM and NMT outputs. Future work could incorporate qualitative case studies or human evaluations to better understand how MT outputs impact the reading experience of child audiences and whether stylistic deficiencies could be mitigated through prompt engineering or fine-tuning techniques.

Lastly, the feature set in this study remains lexical and syntactic-centric, with limited exploration of semantic and discourse-level attributes. Some feature overlaps were also observed, which could introduce redundancy in classification tasks. Future work should incorporate feature correlation analysis and dimensionality reduction methods (e.g., PCA) to refine the feature set and explore network-based approaches for a more holistic view of stylistic variations.

Acknowledgments

We gratefully acknowledge support from the China Scholarship Committee for the Visiting PhD Project (Num. 202406260211). We also thank the three anonymous reviewers for their constructive feedback.

Supplementary material

The supplementary material used in this study is uploaded onto Github `https://github.com/DanielKong1996/CLT_MTsummit`

Sustainability statement

This study primarily utilizes commercial MT engines' APIs during the translation acquisition phase. Due to the nature of these proprietary systems, accurately estimating the associated carbon footprint is challenging. Additionally, the classification and clustering experiments conducted during the machine learning phase of this research require relatively low computational resources. All experiments were performed on a personal laptop, ensuring minimal energy consumption. As a result, the overall environmental impact of this research is expected to be low.

References

Sheila Castilho, Clodagh Mallon, Rahel Meister, and Shengya Yue. 2023. Do online machine translation systems care for context? What about a GPT model? Tampere, Finland. European Association for Machine Translation (EAMT).

Wanxiang Che, Yunlong Feng, Libo Qin, and Ting Liu. 2021. N-LTP: an open-source neural language technology platform for Chinese. In *Proceedings of the 2021 Conference on Empirical Methods in Natural Language Processing: System Demonstrations*, pages 42–49, Online and Punta Cana, Dominican Republic. Association for Computational Linguistics.

Andong Chen, Yuchen Song, Wenxin Zhu, Kehai Chen, Muyun Yang, Tiejun Zhao, and Min zhang. 2025. Evaluating o1-like llms: Unlocking reasoning for translation through comprehensive analysis. *Preprint*, arXiv:2502.11544.

Matthew Y. Chen. 2000. *Tone sandhi: patterns across Chinese dialects*, volume 92. Cambridge University Press.

B. Lee Cooper. 1989. Rhythm 'n' rhymes: character and theme images from children's literature in contemporary recordings, 1950–1985. *Popular Music & Society*.

Joke Daems. 2022. Dutch literary translators' use and perceived usefulness of technology: the role of awareness and attitude. In *Using Technologies for Creative-text Translation*. Routledge.

Joke Daems, Orphée De Clercq, and Lieve Macken. 2017. Translationese and post-editese: how comparable is comparable quality? *Linguistica Antverpiensia, New Series – Themes in Translation Studies*, 16:89–103.

Joke Daems, Paola Ruffo, and Lieve Macken. 2024. Impact of translation workflows with and without MT on textual characteristics in literary translation. In *Proceedings of the 1st Workshop on Creative-text Translation and Technology*, pages 57–64, Sheffield, United Kingdom. European Association for Machine Translation.

Orphée De Clercq, Gert De Sutter, Rudy Loock, Bert Cappelle, and Koen Plevoets. 2021. Uncovering machine translationese using corpus analysis techniques to distinguish between original and machine-translated French. *Translation Quarterly*, (101):21–45.

Guoqi Ding. 2024. Triangulating text relationship in literary retranslation: The Great Gatsby in Chinese. *Digital Scholarship in the Humanities*, (39):849–863.

Maciej Eder. 2015. Rolling stylometry. *Digital Scholarship in the Humanities*, 31(3):457–469.

Maxim Enis and Mark Hopkins. 2024. From LLM to NMT: advancing low-resource machine translation with Claude. *arXiv preprint*.

Michael Farrell. 2018. Machine translation markers in post-edited machine translation output. In *Proceedings of the 40th Conference Translating and the Computer*, pages 50–59.

Anna Fornalczyk-Lipska. 2022. Repetitive or innovative? Children's literature in translation as the main focus of B.A. and M.A. theses. *Journal of Research in Higher Education*, 6:38–51.

Boer Fu. 2022. Contrast preservation in mandarin R-suffixation: a comparative study of beijing and liaoning dialects. *Glossa: a Journal of General Linguistics*, 7(1).

Ana Guerberof-Arenas and Antonio Toral. 2024. To be or not to be. *Target. International Journal of Translation Studies*, 36(2):215–244.

James Luke Hadley, Kristiina Taivalkoski-Shilov, Carlos S. C. Teixeira, and Antonio Toral. 2022. *Using Technologies for Creative-Text Translation*. Taylor & Francis.

Maya Hickmann. 2003. *Children's discourse: person, space, and time across languages*. Cambridge University Press, Cambridge, UK.

Wei Huang and Haitao Liu. 2009. Application of quantitative characteristics of Chinese genres in text clustering [In Chinese]. *Computer Engineering and Applications*, 45(29):25–27, 33.

Yue Jiang and Jiang Niu. 2022. A corpus-based search for machine translationese in terms of discourse coherence. *Across Languages and Cultures*, 23(2):148–166.

Wenxiang Jiao, Wenxuan Wang, Jen-tse Huang, Xing Wang, and Zhaopeng Tu. 2023. Is ChatGPT a good translator? A preliminary study. *arXiv preprint arXiv:2301.08745*, 1(10).

Tom Kocmi, Eleftherios Avramidis, Rachel Bawden, Ondřej Bojar, Anton Dvorkovich, Christian Federmann, Mark Fishel, Markus Freitag, Thamme Gowda, Roman Grundkiewicz, Barry Haddow, Marzena Karpinska, Philipp Koehn, Benjamin Marie, Christof Monz, Kenton Murray, Masaaki Nagata, Martin Popel, Maja Popović, Mariya Shmatova, Steinthór Steingrímsson, and Vilém Zouhar. 2024. Findings of the WMT24 general machine translation shared task: the LLM era is here but MT is not solved yet. In *Proceedings of the Ninth Conference on Machine Translation*, pages 1–46, Miami, Florida, USA. Association for Computational Linguistics.

Gillian Lathey. 2015. *Translating children's literature*. Routledge, London.

Lei Lei, Yaoyu Wei, and Kanglong Liu. 2024. AlphaReadabilityChinese: a tool for the measurement of readability in Chinese texts and its applications. *Foreign Languages and Their Teaching*, 46(1):83–93.

Gerard Lynch and Carl Vogel. 2018. The translator's visibility: detecting translatorial fingerprints in contemporaneous parallel translations. *Computer Speech & Language*, 52:79–104.

Lieve Macken. 2024. Machine translation meets large language models: evaluating ChatGPT's ability to automatically post-edit literary texts. In *Proceedings of the 1st Workshop on Creative-text Translation and Technology*, pages 65–81, Sheffield, United Kingdom. European Association for Machine Translation.

Lorenzo Mastropierro. 2022. The avoidance of repetition in translation: a multifactorial study of repeated reporting verbs in the Italian translation of the harry potter series. In *Advances in Corpus Applications in Literary and Translation Studies*, pages 138–157. Routledge.

Joss Moorkens, Antonio Toral, Sheila Castilho, and Andy Way. 2018. Translators' perceptions of literary post-editing using statistical and neural machine translation. *Translation Spaces*, 7(2):240–262.

Esther Ploeger, Huiyuan Lai, Rik Noord, and Antonio Toral. 2024. Towards tailored recovery of lexical diversity in literary machine translation.

T. Puurtinen. 2003. Genre-specific features of translationese? Linguistic differences between translated and non-translated finnish children's literature. *Literary and Linguistic Computing*, 18(4):389–406.

Simon Päpcke, Thomas Weitin, Katharina Herget, Anastasia Glawion, and Ulrik Brandes. 2022. Stylometric similarity in literary corpora: non-authorship clustering and*Deutscher novellenschatz*. *Digital Scholarship in the Humanities*, 38(1):277–295.

Md. Mostafizer Rahman, Ariful Islam Shiplu, and Yutaka Watanobe. 2024. CommentClass: a robust ensemble machine learning model for comment classification. *International Journal of Computational Intelligence Systems*, 17(1):184.

Paola Ruffo. 2022. Collecting literary translators' narratives: towards a new paradigm for technological innovation in literary translation. In *Using Technologies for Creative-text Translation*. Routledge.

Jan Rybicki. 2025. Can machine translation of literary texts fool stylometry? *Digital Scholarship in the Humanities*, page fqaf010.

Kristiina Taivalkoski-Shilov. 2018. Ethical issues regarding machine(-assisted) translation of literary texts. *Perspectives*, 27(5):689–703.

Deborah Tannen. 1989. *Talking voices: repetition, dialogue, and imagery in conversational discourse*. Cambridge University Press, Cambridge, UK.

Antonio Toral. 2019. Post-editese: an exacerbated translationese. *arXiv preprint arXiv:1907.00900*.

Antonio Toral and Andy Way. 2014. Is machine translation ready for literature. In *Proceedings of Translating and the Computer 36*, London, UK. AsLing.

Antonio Toral and Andy Way. 2015. Machine-assisted translation of literary text: a case study. *Translation Spaces*, 4(2):240–267.

Antonio Toral and Andy Way. 2018. What level of quality can Neural Machine Translation attain on literary text? In Joss Moorkens, Sheila Castilho, Federico Gaspari, and Stephen Doherty, editors, *Translation Quality Assessment: from Principles to Practice*, Machine Translation: Technologies and Applications, pages 263–287. Springer International Publishing, Cham.

Jan Van Coillie and Jack McMartin, editors. 2020. *Children's literature in translation: texts and contexts*. Leuven University Press.

V. Volansky, N. Ordan, and S. Wintner. 2013. On the features of translationese. *Digital Scholarship in the Humanities*, 30(1):98–118.

Matthijs J. Warrens and Hanneke van der Hoef. 2022. Understanding the adjusted rand index and other partition comparison indices based on counting object pairs. *Journal of Classification*, 39(3):487–509.

Andy Way, Andrew Rothwell, and Roy Youdale. 2023. Why literary translators should embrace translation technology. *Tradumàtica Tecnologies De La Traducció*, pages 87–102.

Xu Xu and Jiayin Li. 2020. Concreteness/abstractness ratings for two-character chinese words in MELD-SCH. *PLOS ONE*, 15(6):e0232133.

Xiaomin Zhang, Haidee Kotze (Kruger), and Jing Fang. 2019. Explicitation in children's literature translated from English to Chinese: a corpus-based study of personal pronouns. *Perspectives*, 28(5):717–736.

Meijuan Zhao, Lay Hoon Ang, Sabariah Md Rashid, and Florence Haw Ching Toh. 2022. Translating narrative space in children's fiction bronze and sunflower from Chinese to English. *Sage Open*, 12(1):21582440211068498.

Anna Čermáková. 2018. Translating children's literature: some insights from corpus stylistics. *Ilha Do Desterro*, 71:117–133.

A LLM prompt

The engineered prompt is originally drafted in Chinese, as follows:

你是一位专精于儿童文学翻译与创作的资深译者，你的任务是将 J.M. Barrie 的《Peter Pan》翻译成富有创造力的中文版本。这不仅是一次普通的翻译，而是一种"创译"——你的目标是保留原文的幻想色彩和情感基调，同时使译文更加符合中文儿童的阅读习惯，充满趣味性和文学感染力。

请遵循以下创译原则：

- 情感与想象力再现：保持原著的童话氛围，使译文生动、富有画面感，如必要可调整句式，使其更具表现力。

- 符合儿童语言习惯：采用简练、口语化、充满韵律感的表达方式，避免生硬直译。可适当使用拟声词、叠词、押韵句式等。

- 文化适配：调整可能不易理解的文化元素，使其符合中文语境，但同时保留原作的神秘感和奇幻感。

- 角色个性化语言：确保各个角色的独特特点能在译文中得以体现。

- 增添文学趣味：适当运用修辞（比喻、拟人、夸张等），调整句式，使故事更具节奏感，增强朗读时的感染力。

请翻译以下《彼得潘》片段，并确保符合上述原则: [原文]

English Translation:

You are a seasoned translator and writer specializing in children's literature. Your task is to create a highly creative Chinese adaptation of J.M. Barrie's *Peter Pan*. This is not merely a literal translation but a transcreation - your goal is to preserve the whimsical essence and emotional tone of the original while making the text more engaging and accessible for Chinese children ensuring it is rich in imaginative appeal and literary charm

Guiding Principles for Transcreation:

- Emotional and Imaginative Recreation: Maintain the fairy-tale atmosphere of the original, making the translation vivid and evocative. Feel free to adjust sentence structures to enhance expressiveness.

- Child-Friendly Language: Use concise, rhythmic, and conversational expressions, avoiding rigid literal translation. Incorporate onomatopoeia, reduplication, rhyming phrases, and other playful linguistic elements as appropriate.

- Cultural Adaptation: Modify cultural references that may be difficult for Chinese readers to grasp, ensuring they fit the Chinese linguistic and cultural context while preserving the mystical and fantastical essence of the original.

- Character-Specific Speech: Ensure that each character's unique personality and speech style are well reflected in the translation.

- Enhanced Literary Appeal: Utilize figurative language (e.g., metaphors, personification, hyperbole) and varied sentence structures to enrich the storytelling, improve readability, and enhance the rhythm and emotional impact, particularly when read aloud.

Please translate the following excerpt from Peter Pan while adhering to these principles: [text]

B Feature set in summary

A summary list of features used in the study is in Table 3.

C Selected features used in experiments

A summary list of significant features used in different experiments is in Table 4.

D Supplementary figures

Figure 1 illustrates pair-wised classification results among HTs, NMTs, and LLMs groups.

Figure 2 shows the clustering results.

Figure 3 illustrates ratio of conjunction words, and the ratio of the 1-word-gram-然后 between HTs vs. MTs, and NMTs vs. LLMs.

Figure 4 presents ratio of 1-word-gram-一样 between HTs vs. MTs, and NMTs vs. LLMs, and the distribution ratio of "像……一样" in all texts.

Figure 5 illustrates generic features between HTs vs. MTs, and NMTs vs. LLMs.

Figure 6 shows CTT-specific features between HTs vs. MTs, and NMTs vs. LLMs.

Figure 7 mainly illustrates the distribution of six key features among seven LLMs.

Figure 8 shows an example of the phrase "像...一样" drawn from actual concordance.

Feature level	Sub level	Total	Feature instances
Generic textual features	Lexical	69	STTR, MTLD, noun, verb, content words, idioms ...
	Syntactical	26	WordsPerSent, QuestionSent, MDD, AvgChildrenPerNode...
	Readability	16	lexical_richness, Concreteness score, AvgConcrete ...
	N-grams	309	N_word_gram, N_PoS_gram, N = 1 - 3 ...
CTT-specific features	Repetition	7	ratio_AA, ratio_ABAB, ratio_AAA, ratio_AABB...
	Rhythm	10	Open Syllable Ratio, Rhyme Density, Rhyme Ratio ...
	Translatability	5	completeness, foreignness, code_switching, untranslatable ...
	Miscellaneous	5	ratio_onomatopoeia, ratio_StrongModifier, ratio_er_suffix ...

Table 3: Summary of features used in this study. Due to space constraints, only representative feature instances are listed, with "..." indicating additional features available in the full list (see supplementary materials). Feature names shortened for formatting when necessary.

Groups	Generic features	Specific features
HTs vs. MTs	Ratio_conjunction	foreignness_ratio
	word_1gram_然后	switching_ratio
	word_1gram_一样	ratio_er_suffix
	word_1gram_它们	ratio_StrSentMdfyr
	ratio_adverb	ratio_aabb
	ratio_ContentWords	ratio_AA
NMTs vs. LLMs	word_1gram_没有	code_switching_ratio
	pos_2gram_ws	foreignness_ratio
	ratio_dscrptW	ratio_StrSentMdfyr
	ratio_adverb	ratio_AA
	POB	-
	ratio_prep	-

Table 4: Summary of significant features used in different experiments. 6 features in each sub-categories are selected from top-40 salient features, with "-" mark representing no more features in this category are found in the top-40. Feature names shortened for formatting when necessary.

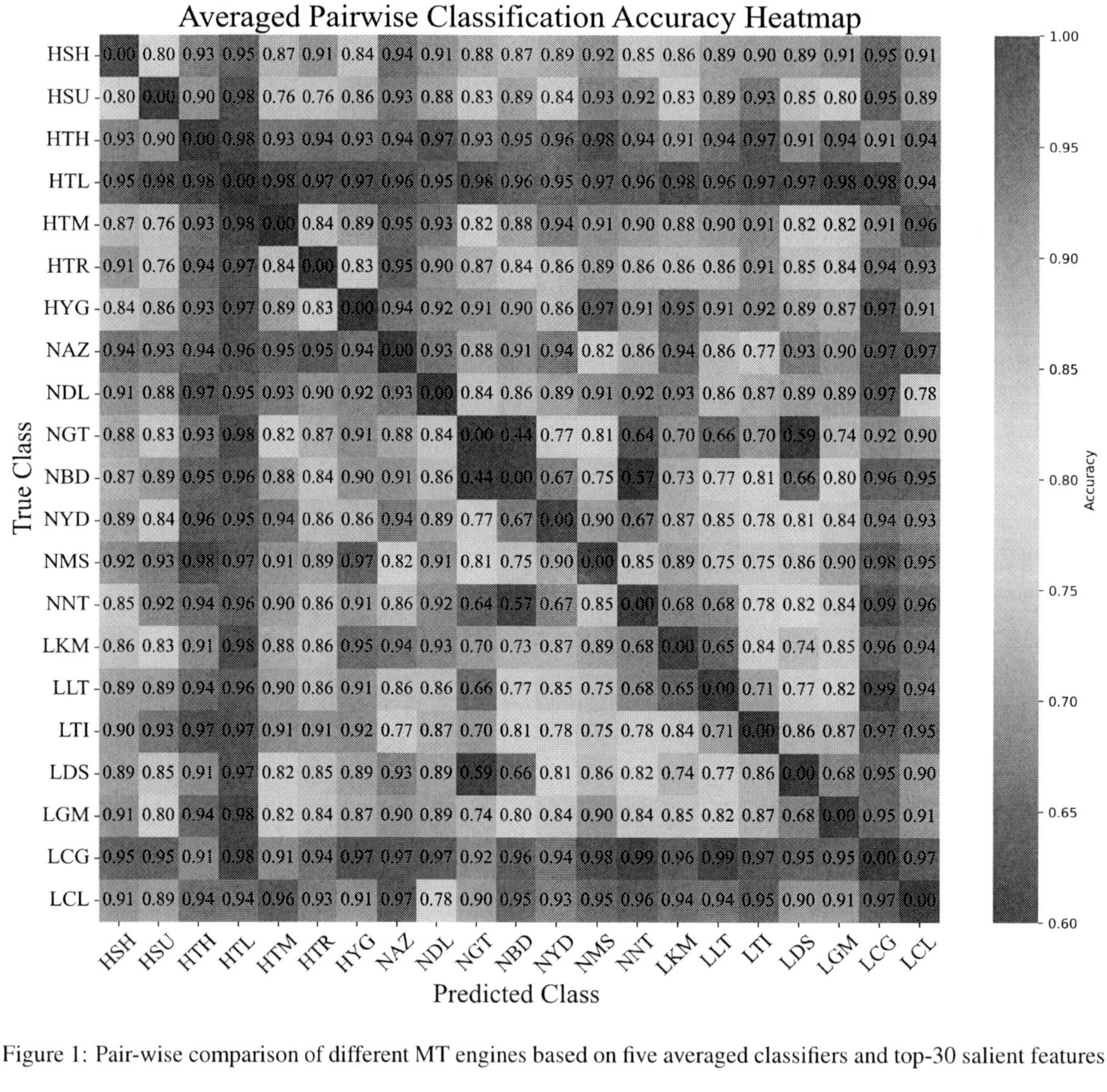

Figure 1: Pair-wise comparison of different MT engines based on five averaged classifiers and top-30 salient features

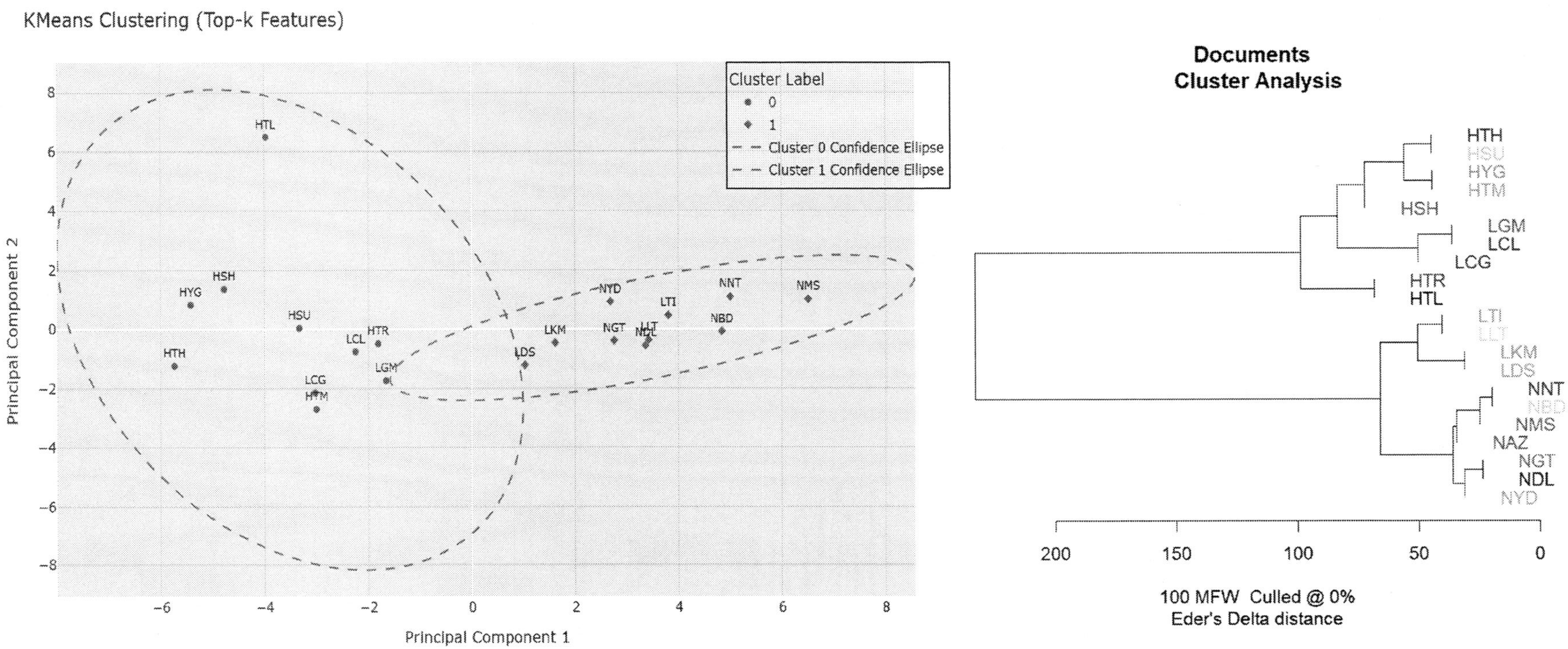

Figure 2: Left: using Top-30 features in K-means clustering with $k = 2$, where the true labels are set as HTs = 0 and MTs = 1. ARI is 0.4873, and the confidence ellipse is set at 0.7. Right: hierarchical clustering using the Stylo package with 100 MFWs and Eder's delta as the distance measure.

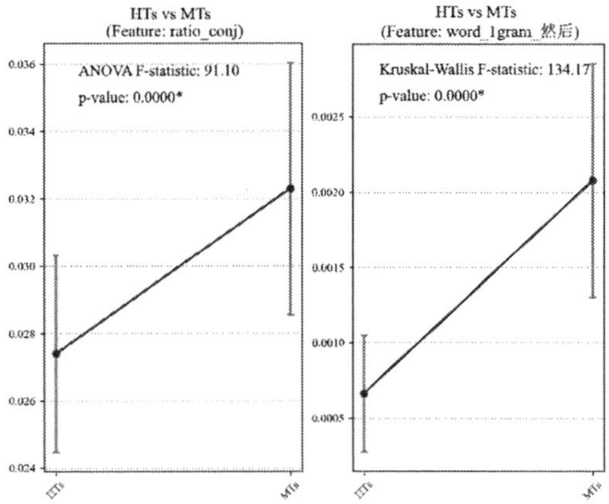

Figure 3: Generic differences between HTs and MTs. The left panel compares ratio of conjunction words, while the right panel examines ratio of the 1-word-gram-然后

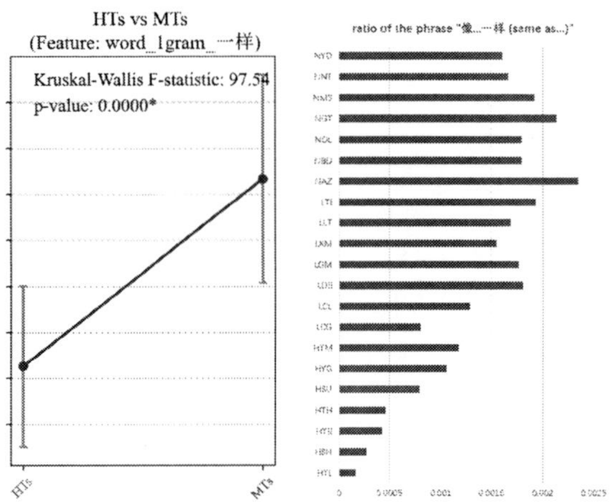

Figure 4: The left panel compares ratio of 1-word-gram-一样, while the right panel shows the distribution ratio of "像. . . 一样" in all texts.

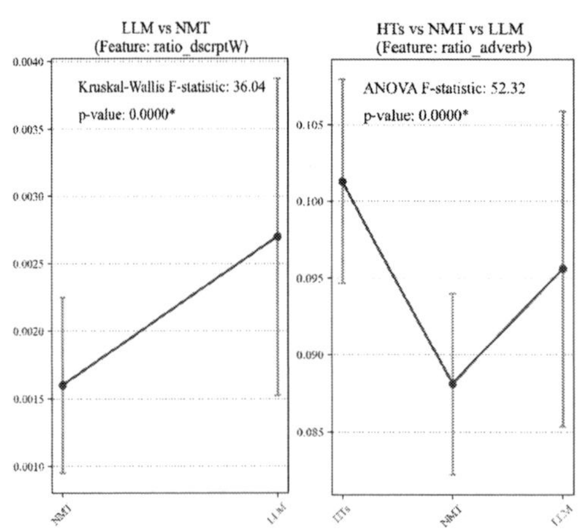

Figure 5: Generic differences between HTs and MTs. The left panel compares ratio of descriptive words, while the right panel examines ratio of the adverbs among HTs, NMTs and LLMs.

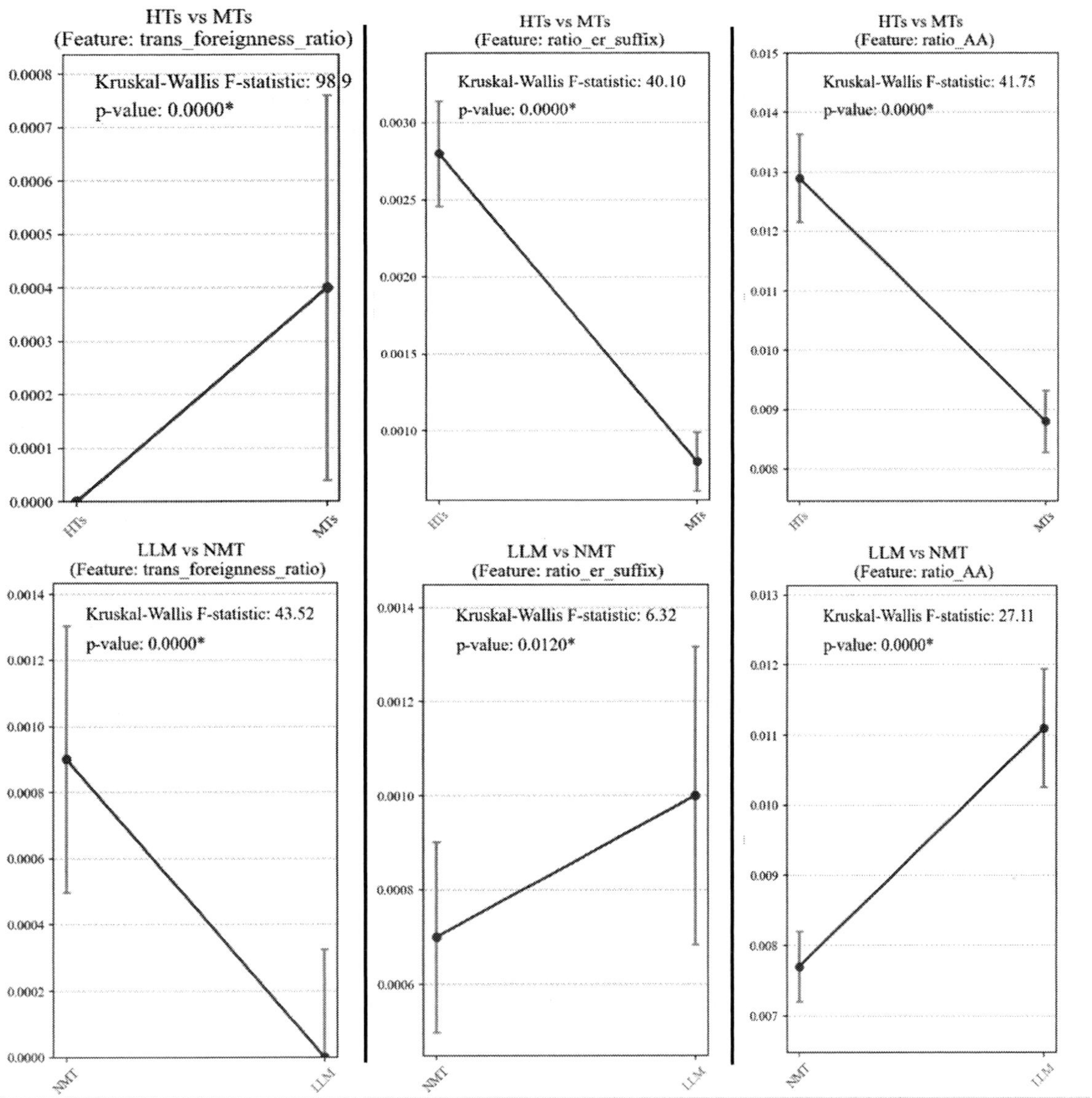

Figure 6: Feature distribution comparisons between different translation groups. The left column presents the differences in *trans_foreignness_ratio*; the middle column shows variations in *ratio_er_suffix*; and the right column illustrates the differences in AA-pattern repetitive expression.

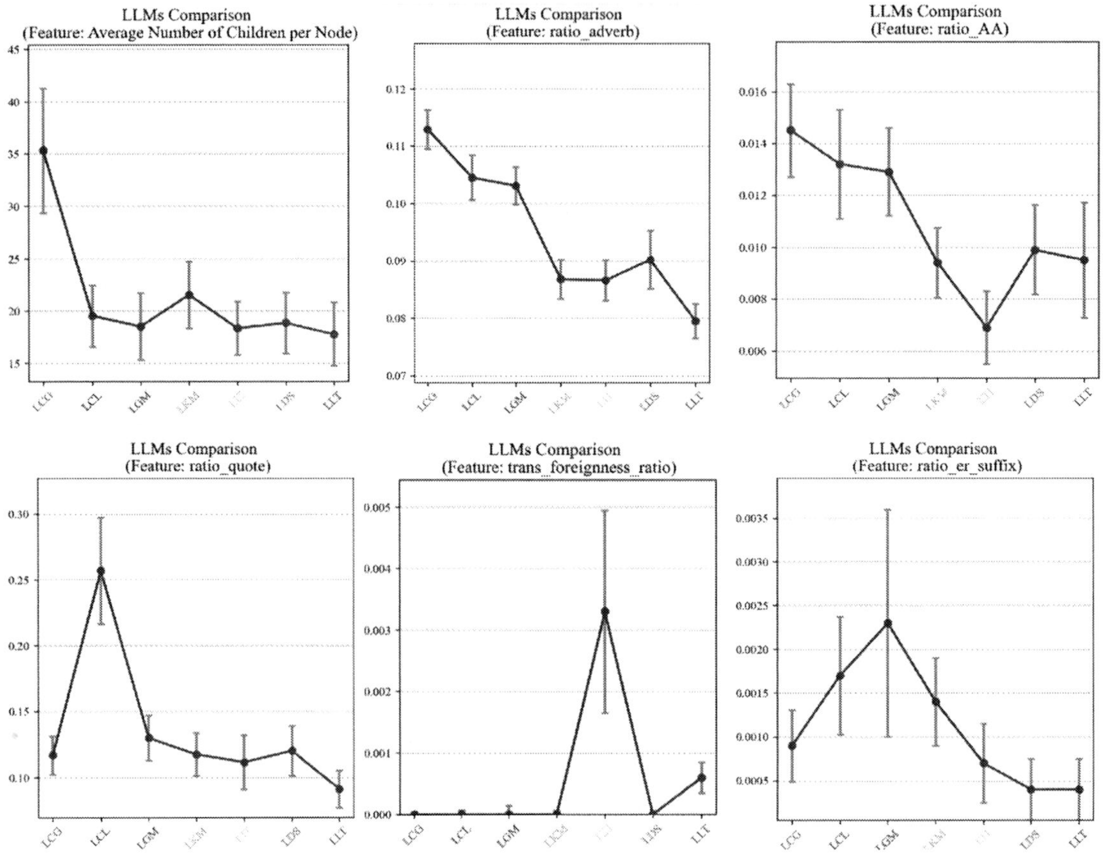

Figure 7: Comparison of key linguistic features across seven different LLMs. The top-left plot shows differences in *Average Number of Children per Node*; the top-middle *ratio_adverb*; the top-right *ratio_AA*. The bottom-left plot presents differences in *ratio_quote*; the bottom-middle *trans_foreignness_ratio*; the bottom-right *ratio_er_suffix*.

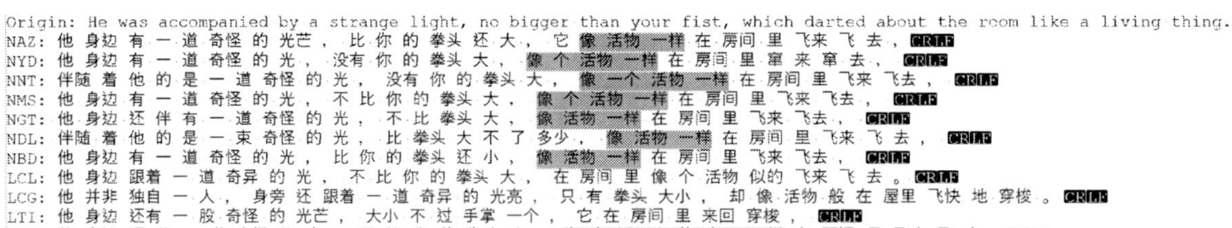
Origin: He was accompanied by a strange light, no bigger than your fist, which darted about the room like a living thing.
NAZ: 他 身边 有 一 道 奇怪 的 光芒 ， 比 你 的 拳头 还 大 ， 它 像 活物 一样 在 房间 里 飞来 飞 去 ， CRLF
NYD: 他 身边 有 一 道 奇怪 的 光 ， 没有 你 的 拳头 大 ， 像 个 活物 一样 在 房间 里 窜 来 窜 去 ， CRLF
NNT: 伴随 着 他 的 是 一 道 奇怪 的 光 ， 没有 你 的 拳头 大 ， 像 一个 活物 一样 在 房间 里 飞来 飞去 ， CRLF
NMS: 他 身边 有 一 道 奇怪 的 光 ， 不 比 你 的 拳头 大 ， 像 个 活物 一样 在 房间 里 飞来 飞去 ， CRLF
NGT: 他 身边 还 伴 有 一 道 奇怪 的 光 ， 不 比 拳头 大 ， 像 活物 一样 在 房间 里 飞来 飞去 ， CRLF
NDL: 伴随 着 他 的 是 一 束 奇怪 的 光 ， 比 拳头 大 不 了 多少 ， 像 活物 一样 在 房间 里 飞来 飞 去 ， CRLF
NBD: 他 身边 有 一 道 奇怪 的 光 ， 比 你 的 拳头 还 小 ， 像 活物 一样 在 房间 里 飞来 飞去 ， CRLF
LCL: 他 身边 跟着 一 道 奇异 的 光 ， 不 比 你 的 拳头 大 ， 在 房间 里 像 个 活物 似的 飞来 飞 去 。 CRLF
LCG: 他 并非 独自 一 人 ， 身旁 还 跟着 一 道 奇异 的 光亮 ， 只 有 拳头 大小 ， 却 像 活物 般 在 屋里 飞快 地 穿梭 。 CRLF
LTI: 他 身边 还有 一 股 奇怪 的 光芒 ， 大小 不 过 手掌 一个 ， 它 在 房间 里 来回 穿梭 ， CRLF
LLT: 他 身边 闪 着 一 道 奇怪 的 光 ， 不 比 你 的 拳头 大 ， 像 个 活生生 的 东西 一样 在 房间 里 飞来 飞 去 ， CRLF
LKM: 他 身边 伴随 着 一 束 奇异 的 光芒 ， 那 光束 不 比 你 的 拳头 大 ， 它 在 房间 里 像 活物 一样 四处 飞 蹿 ， CRLF
LGM: 他 身边 带 着 一 盏 奇怪 的 光 ， 不 比 你 的 拳头 大 ， 在 房间 里 像 个 活物 一样 飞来 飞 去 ， CRLF
HYG: 伴随 着 他 的 ， 还有 一 团 奇异 的 光 ， 那 光 还 没有 你 的 拳头 那么 大 ， 它 像 一个 活物 在 房间 里 四处 乱 飞 。 CRLF
HTR: 他 带有 一 种 奇怪 的 光 。 不 比 你 的 拳头 大 ， 像 个 活 的 东西 那样 在 房间 里 窜 来 窜 去 ； CRLF
HTM: 跟 他 在 一起 的 还有 一 道 奇异 的 光 ， 跟 你 的 拳头 差不多 大 ， 像 一个 活物 一样 在 房间 里 蹿动 ， CRLF
HTL: 陪 着 他 来 的 还有 一 颗 奇异 的 火亮 ， 不见得 比 你 的 头 大 ， 像 是 活 东西 似的 在 屋里 乱 飞 ， CRLF
HTH: 男孩 身边 有 一 团 奇怪 的 光 ， 比 拳头 大 不 了 多少 ， 那 团 光 在 房间 里 横冲直撞 ， 像 是 个 活物 。 CRLF
HSU: 紧跟着 他 的 ， 是 一 团 怪异 的 光 ， 一 团 还 没有 拳头 大 的 光 ， 像 个 有 生命 的 活物 一样 ， 在 房间 里面 四处 乱 飞 。 CRLF
HSH: 与 他 相伴 的 还有 一 道 奇妙 的 光 ， 那 光 并 不 比 你 的 拳头 大 ， 宛如 一个 精灵 在 房间 里 横冲直撞 ， CRLF

Figure 8: Actual concordance in the corpus of the feature “像...... 一样”. Highlights by matching regular expression “像[一-龟]+一样”.

Author Index

The Second Workshop on Creative-text Translation and Technology (CTT) organisers gratefully acknowledge the support from the following sponsors.

INTERACT: Interdisciplinary research network on language contact research. Interact is funded by the Research Foundation Flanders (FWO) with grant number W002220N.

The Faculty of Arts and Philosophy of Ghent University (UGent).

Association for Computational Linguistics
209 N. Eighth Street
Stroudsburg, Pennsylvania 18360

ISBN 979-8-3313-2671-5

9 798331 326715

CURRAN ASSOCIATES INC.
proceedings.com